UNCLASSIFIED

(U) The FBI: Protecting the Homeland in the 21st Century

(U) Report of the Congressionally-directed

(U) 9/11 Review Commission

To

(U) The Director of the Federal Bureau of Investigation

By

(U) Commissioners

Bruce Hoffman
Edwin Meese III
Timothy J. Roemer

(U) March 2015

UNCLASSIFIED

UNCLASSIFIED

(U) The FBI: Protecting the Homeland in the 21st Century

(U) Report of the Congressionally-directed

(U) 9/11 Review Commission

To

(U) The Director of the Federal Bureau of Investigation

(U) By

Bruce Hoffman   Edwin Meese III   Timothy J. Roemer

UNCLASSIFIED

(U) TABLE OF CONTENTS

(U) INTRODUCTION
THE FBI 9/11 REVIEW COMMISSION

(U) The FBI 9/11 Review Commission was established in January 2014 pursuant to a congressional mandate.[1] The United States Congress directed the Federal Bureau of Investigation (FBI, or the "Bureau") to create a commission with the expertise and scope to conduct a "comprehensive external review of the implementation of the recommendations related to the FBI that were proposed by the National Commission on Terrorist Attacks Upon the United States (commonly known as the 9/11 Commission)."[2] The Review Commission was tasked specifically to report on:

1. *An assessment of the progress made, and challenges in implementing the recommendations of the 9/11 Commission that are related to the FBI.*

2. *An analysis of the FBI's response to trends of domestic terror attacks since September 11, 2001, including the influence of domestic radicalization.*

3. *An assessment of any evidence not known to the FBI that was not considered by the 9/11 Commission related to any factors that contributed in any manner to the terrorist attacks of September 11, 2001.*

4. *Any additional recommendations with regard to FBI intelligence sharing and counterterrorism policy.[3]*

(U) The Review Commission was funded by Congress in Fiscal Years 2013, 2014, and 2015 (FY13, FY14, and FY15) budgets that provided for operations for one-year ending with the submission of its review to the Director of the FBI. The enabling legislation also required the FBI Director to report to the Congressional committees of jurisdiction on the findings and recommendations resulting from this review.[4]

(U) In late November 2013, the FBI Director, in consultation with Congress, appointed three commissioners to what became known as the 9/11 Review Commission: former Attorney General Edwin Meese, former Congressman and Ambassador Tim Roemer, and Professor and counterterrorism expert Bruce Hoffman of Georgetown University. In February 2014, the

---

1 (U) The relevant legislation includes: Title II, Div. B, *Consolidated and Further Continuing Appropriations Act, 2013*, P.L. 113-6 (March 26, 2013) (Salaries and Expenses, Federal Bureau of Investigation) and accompanying Explanatory Statement, S1287, S1305 (March 11, 2013); Title II, Div. B, *Consolidated Appropriations Act, 2014*, P.L. 113-76 (January 17, 2014) (Salaries and Expenses, Federal Bureau of Investigation) and accompanying Explanatory Statement, H475, H512 (January 15, 2014); Title II, Div. B, *Consolidated and Further Continuing Appropriations Act, 2015*, P.L. 113-235 (December 16, 2014) (Salaries and Expenses, Federal Bureau of Investigation) and accompanying Explanatory Statement, H9307, H9346 (December 11, 2014).
2 (U) Explanatory Statement accompanying P.L. 113-6 at S1305 (March 11, 2013).
3 (U) Ibid.
4 (U) Title II, Div. B, *Consolidated and Further Continuing Appropriations Act, 2013*, P.L. 113-6 (March 26, 2013) (Salaries and Expenses, Federal Bureau of Investigation) and accompanying Explanatory Statement, S1287, S1305 (March 11, 2013).

commissioners appointed as Executive Director, John Gannon, former Central Intelligence Agency (CIA) Deputy Director for Intelligence and ex-Chairman of the National Intelligence Council.

(U) The Executive Director, working with the commissioners and coordinating with the Bureau, assembled a staff that eventually numbered 12 individuals: two former senior intelligence officers, one former assistant US Attorney (and previously a Senior Counsel on the original 9/11 Commission) detailed from the MITRE Corporation, one trial attorney detailed from the Department of Justice (DOJ), one retired senior Congressional (intelligence committees) staffer, two senior counterterrorism experts detailed from the RAND Corporation, two senior analysts detailed from the Defense Intelligence Agency (DIA), two personnel detailed from the FBI, and one former federal and military prosecutor currently in private practice in Washington.[5]

(U) The Review Commission produced a conceptual framework to guide the staff's review and production of a report fully addressing its legislative mandate. The framework contained five objectives around which four staff teams were organized. The commissioners presented this framework in testimony before the Commerce, Justice, Science, and Related Agencies Subcommittee of the House Appropriations Committee on March 26, 2014.

(U) Four team leaders were identified and assigned to lead the specific lines of inquiry stated in the commissioners' March Congressional testimony: (1) a baseline assessment of where the Bureau is today in its transition to a threat-based, intelligence-driven organization and "the development of an institutional culture imbued with deep expertise in intelligence and national security;" (2) an analysis of institutional lessons learned and practical takeaways from the assessment of five high-profile counterterrorism cases that occurred in the past six years; (3) an evaluation of the FBI's current state of preparedness to address the rapidly evolving, global threat environment of the next decade—including escalating cyber intrusions, proliferating numbers of foreign fighters, and increasingly adaptive terrorist activities; and (4) an examination of the Bureau's current and future need for closer collaboration and information sharing with strategic partners inside and outside government, and with other federal, state, local, tribal, and international counterparts. In addition, the Review Commission produced a fifth chapter summarizing its effort to identify any evidence now known to the FBI that was not considered by the 9/11 Commission related to any factors that contributed in any manner to the terrorist attacks of September 11, 2001.

---

5 (U) The staff, hired over several months, consisted of seven full-time and five part-time employees. Delays in hiring slowed the progress of the review, but never halted it. All staff members reported administratively to the FBI. The three commissioners, the executive director, and three of the staff members worked under personal services contracts (PSCs), three staff members served pursuant to Intergovernmental Personnel Agreements (IPAs), with the remaining staff under rotational or specialized agreements with the FBI. With regard to access, we experienced a "pull system"—we received what we asked for—but the responsiveness and collaborative spirit of our two substantive FBI liaison officers, Elizabeth Callahan and Jacqueline Maguire, provided us invaluable access to key people and relevant data that enabled us to produce an objective, comprehensive, and constructive review. They also conducted, in collaboration with the commission staff, an exhaustive fact-based review of the draft report that improved its accuracy and clarity.

4

(U) Scope of Effort

(U) The Review Commission received over 60 extensive briefings on a broad range of subjects from the FBI headquarters' divisions. A comprehensive list of the briefing topics can be found in Appendix A.[6] No briefing requests were denied. The Review Commission made numerous document and information requests and in turn generated internal documents and Memoranda for the Record. The Review Commission conducted meetings at the training and science and technology facilities at Quantico, Virginia, to gain firsthand knowledge regarding the changes to the training program as well as developments in the scientific realm.

(U) The Review Commission interviewed over 30 Bureau and United States Intelligence Community (USIC) officials and other experts, including former FBI Director Robert Mueller, Director of National Intelligence (DNI) James Clapper, Director of CIA John Brennan, former DIA Director Lt. Gen. (Ret.) Michael Flynn, former National Counterterrorism Center (NCTC) Directors Michael Leiter and Matthew Olson, Customs and Border Protection (CBP) Commissioner Gil Kerlikowske, Transportation Security Administration (TSA) Administrator John Pistole, and had several meetings with current FBI Director James Comey. A comprehensive list of the interviewees can be found in Appendix B.[7]

(U) The Review Commission traveled to eight field offices (Washington, Boston, Denver, Detroit, Minneapolis, Chicago, San Diego, and New York) interviewing key personnel, including members of counterterrorism squads, analytic units, Joint Terrorism Task Force members, field office leadership, and key external partners such as local police chiefs. The Review Commission also visited six Legal Attaché (LEGAT) posts (Ottawa, Beijing, Manila, Singapore, London, and Madrid) for extensive discussions and meetings with the LEGATs (and members of his or her team), ambassadors, relevant members of the country teams, and participated in outside meetings with the Bureau's key foreign liaison partners.

(U) The Review Commission and staff selected field office and LEGAT visits based on issues related to the cases reviewed, on significant US border issues, on important internal US and foreign collaborative relationships, and on specific local or regional counterterrorism challenges. The Review Commission also interviewed at Headquarters the LEGATS from Abu Dhabi, Ankara, Hong Kong, Kiev, Nairobi, and Tel Aviv.

(U) The Review Commission received outstanding support from Headquarters divisions, from the field offices, and from the LEGAT posts in response to its extensive requirements. At Headquarters, Elizabeth Callahan and Jacqueline Maguire, who were in daily contact with the staff, deserve special mention for their unfailing positive response to the Review Commission's steady flow of requirements for briefings, meetings, and documents. We are also grateful to Patrick Findlay, who provided guidance on legal, contracts, and logistical issues. The commissioners also wish to thank Sarah Maksoud, a graduate student in the Security Studies Program at Georgetown University, for her generous preparation of exceptionally useful summaries of relevant unclassified reports.

---

6 (U) A complete list of briefings and meetings is contained in Appendix A.
7 (U) A complete list of interviews conducted is contained in Appendix B.

(U) It is important to acknowledge the report's limitations. The Review Commission took several months to assemble staff and hire personnel, due to bureaucratic, clearance, and other unpredictable and administrative issues. The staff worked for 11 months to address an extremely broad and challenging mandate from Congress, which required continuous focus on the most challenging issues. In particular, the staff devoted extensive time to the Bureau's intelligence collection and analysis programs, its collaboration and information sharing practices, and its strategic planning and implementation. The staff also derived practical lessons from recent FBI cases.

(U) 9/11 Commission Recommendations

(U) The Review Commission recognized that its report must move beyond the baseline of 2004, when the country was at the peak of launching reforms to prevent another catastrophic terrorist attack on the Homeland, to a decade later when those enacted reforms have arguably helped to prevent another such attack. Many of the findings and recommendations in this report will not be new to the FBI. The Bureau is already taking steps to address them. In 2015, however, the FBI faces an increasingly complicated and dangerous global threat environment that will demand an accelerated commitment to reform. Everything is moving faster. The box below summarizes the Bureau's response to the recommendations of the 9/11 Commission, a good place to start.

(U) The FBI's Response to the 9/11 Commission's Recommendations[8]

(U) Overarching Recommendation:

(U) "A specialized and integrated national security workforce should be established at the FBI consisting of agents, analysts, linguists, and surveillance specialists who are recruited, trained, rewarded, and retained to ensure the development of an institutional culture imbued with a deep expertise in intelligence and national security."

(U) *Review Commission Finding*: The Bureau has established comprehensive structures, programs, and policies to build an end-to-end intelligence architecture for intelligence requirements, collection, analysis, production, and dissemination. It has assigned analysts, including reports officers, and human intelligence (HUMINT) collectors to the field. It has introduced a well-conceived, entity-wide threat prioritization process. Intelligence support has been prioritized, though it requires faster progress and deeper execution. Its detailees to other agencies, including the NCTC and the National Intelligence Council (NIC), have had a positive impact. Fundamentally, however, the Review Commission's report highlights a significant gap between the articulated principles of the Bureau's intelligence programs and their effectiveness in practice. The Bureau needs to accelerate its pursuit of its stated goals for intelligence as a matter of increased urgency.

(U) Subordinate Recommendations:

---

8 (U) The 9/11 Commission's recommendations quoted from *The 9/11 Review Commission Report: Final Report of the National Commission on Terrorist Attacks Upon the United States* (*9/11 Commission Report*) (US Government Printing Office, Washington, D.C., 2004): 425-427.

1. (U) "The president, by executive order or directive, should direct the FBI to develop this intelligence cadre."

   (U) *Review Commission Finding*: In the aftermath of the events in 9/11, the FBI had already taken steps to improve and expand its intelligence cadre. However, the FBI was first formally directed to create a Directorate of Intelligence through a November 18, 2004, Presidential Memorandum for the Attorney General (titled "Further Strengthening Federal Bureau of Investigation Capabilities"). [9] The Bureau has responded with the creation of an Executive Assistant Director for Intelligence.

2. (U) "Recognizing that cross-fertilization between the criminal justice and national security disciplines is vital to the success of both missions, all new agents should receive basic training in both areas. Furthermore, new agents should begin their careers with meaningful assignments in both areas."

   (U) *Review Commission Finding*: Subsequent to the 9/11 Commission's recommendations, the FBI re-engineered new agent training to encompass both criminal and national security training and increased the training from 16 weeks to 21 weeks. New agents are required to complete certain developmental tasks that cover foundational skills as well as skills needed for National Security Branch (NSB) and Intelligence functions.

3. (U) "Agents and analysts should then specialize in one of these disciplines and have the option to work such matters for their entire career with the Bureau. Certain advanced training courses and assignments to other intelligence agencies should be required to advance within the national security discipline."

   (U) *Review Commission Finding*: Through the Agent Operational Designation Program (AODP), agents are assigned career path designations in order to increase program-specific and intelligence expertise of agents by providing clear guidance for career progression and high quality, job-relevant training, and developmental opportunities. While the option to choose an area of focus exists for intelligence analysts, for some the development of advanced courses and required interagency rotations their progression in the national security field is still a work in progress. The FBI is engaged in the USIC joint duty program and requires USIC joint duty credit experience for all senior executive positions within the FBI's national security and intelligence components. Its personnel are increasingly enrolled in the certificate and degree awarding programs of the National Intelligence University (NIU). These new efforts must be expedited and encouraged.

4. (U) "In the interest of cross-fertilization, all senior FBI managers, including those working on law enforcement matters, should be certified intelligence officers."

   (U) *Review Commission Finding*: There is a lack of clarity regarding the qualifications of a "certified" intelligence officer as directed by the original 9/11 Commission. The FBI Intelligence Officer Certification (FIOC) program was established in response to the recommendation; however, it is currently under suspension and review for its effectiveness in promoting the FBI's goals for integrated professional development. To broaden intelligence experience, the FBI is

---

9 (U) "Memorandum for the Attorney General: Further Strengthening Federal Bureau of Investigation Capabilities" November 18, 2004.

creating intelligence operations training and education for the workforce, scheduled to be rolled out in FY15 and FY16.

5. (U) "The FBI should fully implement a recruiting, hiring, and selection process for agents and analysts that enhances its ability to target and attract individuals with educational and professional backgrounds in intelligence, international relations, language, technology, and other relevant skills."

   (U) *Review Commission Finding*: The Bureau has made a concerted effort over the past decade to upgrade its skills-based recruitment for its increasingly complex missions, including cyber. This effort will need to be accelerated to meet the diverse personnel and technology challenges ahead.

6. (U) "The FBI should institute the integration of analysts, agents, linguists, and surveillance personnel in the field so that a dedicated team approach is brought to bear on national security intelligence operations."

   (U) *Review Commission Finding:* In response to the need for greater integration of agents and analysts and to provide a firm foundation of working on a team, over the past decade the FBI instituted some shared training for new analysts and agents to integrate them together at the beginning of their FBI careers. Once deployed to the field, many of these analysts have been embedded in operational squads in the field, though their work favors support to tactical and case work at the expense of strategic analysis. The FBI launched a more structured Integrated Curriculum Initiative (ICI) in 2014, with the primary goal to develop a comprehensive basic training program for new agents and analysts that teaches them to operate in a threat-based, intelligence-driven, operationally-focused environment. According to data provided by the FBI, the newly developed curriculum will be the foundation for the FBI's 20-week Basic Field Training Course (BFTC) for new agents and analysts and consist of over 300 hours of integrated training, reinforced with joint practical exercises. The BFTC will be piloted in April 2015, with full implementation to begin in September 2015. Except for the larger field offices, linguists, who are still in short supply, are principally accessed by a virtual system. The Review Commission recognizes this is a challenging process; however, hiring additional linguists and integrating them into operations should be a high priority

7. (U) "Each field office should have an official at the field office's deputy level for national security matters. This individual would have management oversight and ensure that the national priorities are carried out in the field."

   (U) *Review Commission Finding*: Each field office has at least one Assistant Special Agent in Charge (ASAC) responsible for the intelligence program and national security matters. The FBI has further instituted changes to ensure national priorities are carried out in the field through systematic mechanisms such as the Threat Review and Prioritization Process (TRP) and Integrated Program Management (IPM); however, it is unclear the extent to which the program metrics are effective or ensure priorities are addressed.

8. (U) "The FBI should align its budget structure according to its four main programs: intelligence, counterterrorism and counterintelligence, criminal, and criminal justice services—to ensure better transparency on program costs, management of resources, and protection of the intelligence program."

(U) ***Review Commission Finding***: In direct response, the FBI adjusted its budget structure to meet the objectives of the recommendation and further consolidated all national security and intelligence programs under the NSB in 2005. In 2014, the FBI further re-aligned its intelligence program by creating the new Intelligence Branch (IB). It is important to note that sequestration in FY14 severely hindered the FBI's intelligence and national security programs.

9. **(U)** "The FBI should report regularly to Congress in its semiannual program reviews designed to identify whether each field office is appropriately addressing FBI and national program priorities."

   (U) ***Review Commission Finding***: The FBI, according to the data it provided, reports regularly to Congress on these programs through its meetings, testimony, and general oversight process. For example, during the 111th Congress, the FBI presented 15 briefings and participated in two hearings that addressed issues related to national security and intelligence program priorities. During the 112th Congress, the FBI provided 16 briefings and participated in six hearings that addressed these issues. In addition, Congress must actively perform its oversight responsibilities to ensure the implementation of these Review Commission recommendations.

10. **(U)** "The FBI should report regularly to Congress in detail on the qualifications, status, and roles of analysts in the field and at headquarters. Congress should ensure that analysts are afforded training and career opportunities on a par with those offered to analysts in other intelligence community agencies."

    (U) ***Review Commission Finding***: According to data provided to the Review Commission by the FBI, the above-mentioned Congressional briefings and hearings on national security program priorities also addressed issues related to the intelligence program, to include the qualifications, status, and roles of analysts in the field and at headquarters. The Review Commission found that the training and professional status of analysts has improved in recent years. The Intelligence Community Analysis Training and Education Council (ICATEC) in December 2014 found that the FBI's analytic training was on par with CIA, DIA, National Geospatial-Intelligence Agency (NGA), and National Security Agency (NSA). The Review Commission found, however, that access to continuous FBI training, to external education, and to developmental career opportunities lags behind other USIC agencies.

11. **(U)** "The Congress should make sure funding is available to accelerate the expansion of secure facilities in FBI field offices so as to increase their ability to use secure e-mail systems and classified intelligence product exchanges. The Congress should monitor whether the FBI's information-sharing principles are implemented in practice."

    (U) ***Review Commission Finding***: The FBI continues to make progress in acquiring adequate secure facilities for its field offices and LEGAT posts, though it is still behind where it needs to be. It also is investing in IT infrastructure improvements to enhance communications with the USIC and state and local partners. The Review Commission found that the FBI's information sharing practices have progressed markedly, with continuing room for improvement with local law enforcement.

(U) COMMISSIONERS

(U) EDWIN "ED" MEESE III

(U) Ed Meese is currently associated with the Heritage Foundation as the leading think tank's Ronald Reagan Distinguished Fellow Emeritus. In that capacity, Meese oversees special projects and acts as an ambassador for Heritage within the conservative movement. He is also a distinguished visiting fellow at the Hoover Institution at Stanford University in California and lectures, writes, and consults throughout the United States on a variety of subjects. From 1977 to 1981, Meese was a law professor at the University of San Diego, where he also directed the Center for Criminal Justice Policy and Management. From January 1981 to February 1985, Meese held the position of counselor to the President—and functioned as President Reagan's chief policy adviser. Meese then served as Attorney General under President Reagan from 1985-1988. In May 2006, Meese was named a member of the Iraq Study Group and co-authored the group's final December 2006 report. Meese also served on the National War Powers Commission and the Commission for the Evaluation of the National Institute of Justice. Meese has authored several books, including *Leadership, Ethics and Policing, Making America Safer,* and *With Reagan: The Inside Story.* Meese is a retired Colonel in the United States Army Reserve, where he served in the military intelligence and civil affairs branches.

(U) TIM ROEMER

 (U) Tim Roemer, former six-term US representative for Indiana's 3rd congressional district, most recently served as US ambassador to India. He has a strong background in international trade and investment, education policy, and national security.

(U) During his tenure as the lead diplomat in India, Ambassador Roemer was charged with leading one of America's largest diplomatic missions. Under the leadership of President Obama and Secretary of State Hillary Clinton, he was responsible for broadening and deepening the US-India partnership. He oversaw the implementation of several key policies and initiatives, including increasing cooperation, technology transfer and commercial sales in the defense and space industries; signing the Counterterrorism Cooperation Initiative to further expand cooperation in areas such as intelligence and homeland security, border security, money laundering and terrorist financing; and working with the United States to assist India on its Global Center for Nuclear Energy Partnership. He also emphasized commerce and exports, helping move India from America's 25th-largest trading partner to 12th.

(U) Prior to his diplomatic appointment, Ambassador Roemer served for 12 years in the US House of Representatives, where he was deeply engaged in efforts to improve access, standards, and achievement for American education. He was a member of the 9/11 Commission and one of the first members of Congress to advocate for a more dynamic and entrepreneurial Department of Homeland Security. He also served on the Washington Institute's Presidential Task Force on Combating the Ideology of Radical Extremism. Additionally, Ambassador Roemer has served on national commissions and advisory panels and on the board of directors for Oshkosh Corporation.

(U) Known as a consensus-builder and problem-solver, Ambassador Roemer was also president of the Center for National Policy, where he brought together experts and policy-makers to facilitate political cooperation to address critical national security challenges.

(U) Ambassador Roemer has served as a distinguished scholar at George Mason University and has taught at Harvard University's Institute of Politics. He earned a BA degree from the University of California at San Diego and his M.A. and Ph.D. in American government from the University of Notre Dame. He has received distinguished alumnus awards from both schools.

(U) BRUCE HOFFMAN

(U) Professor Bruce Hoffman has been studying terrorism and insurgency for nearly four decades. He is a professor in Georgetown University's Edmund A. Walsh School of Foreign Service where he is also the Director of both the Center for Security Studies and of the Security Studies Program. Professor Hoffman is also a visiting Professor of Terrorism Studies at St. Andrews University, Scotland. He previously held the Corporate Chair in Counterterrorism and Counterinsurgency at the RAND Corporation and was also Director of RAND's Washington, D.C. office. He was Scholar-in-Residence for Counterterrorism at the Central Intelligence Agency between 2004 and 2006; an adviser on counterterrorism to the Office of National Security Affairs, Coalition Provisional Authority, Baghdad, Iraq, in 2004; and from 2004-2005 an adviser on counterinsurgency to the Strategy, Plans, and Analysis Office at Multi-National Forces-Iraq Headquarters, Baghdad. Professor Hoffman was also an adviser to the Iraq Study Group. He is the author of *Inside Terrorism* (2006). His most recent book is *The Evolution of the Global Terrorist Threat: From 9/11 to Osama bin Laden's Death* (2014). *Anonymous Soldiers: The Struggle for Israel, 1917-1947* will be published in 2015.

11

(U) COMMISSION STAFF

(U) EXECUTIVE DIRECTOR

(U) John Gannon served as CIA's Director of European Analysis (1992-1995), as Deputy Director for Intelligence (1995-1997), Assistant Director of Central Intelligence for Analysis and Production (1998-2001), and as Chairman of the National Intelligence Council (1997-2001). After his retirement from CIA in 2001, he served in the White House as the head of the intelligence team standing up the Department of Homeland Security (2002-2003) and later on the Hill as the staff director of the House Select Committee on Homeland Security (2003-2005). In 2004, President George W. Bush awarded him the National Security Medal, the nation's highest intelligence award. Gannon retired from BAE Systems (2005-2012) as President of the Intelligence and Security Sector. He is an adjunct professor at Georgetown University in the Security Studies Program. Gannon is a member of the Board of Visitors of the National Intelligence University. He is a member of the Board of Directors of Voices of September 11th (9/11 families), of the Homeland Security Project, of the National Academies of Science (NAS) Division Committee on Engineering and Physical Sciences, and of the Council on Foreign Relations. Gannon earned his BA in psychology at Holy Cross College, and his M.A. and Ph.D. in history at Washington University in St. Louis. He is a former Naval Officer (retired captain) and Vietnam veteran. He was an elected member of the city council and Chairman of the Planning Commission in his home town of Falls Church, Virginia.

(Staff Members in Alphabetical Order)

(U) Kim Cragin, MPP, Ph.D., is a senior political scientist at the RAND Corporation focusing on terrorism-related issues. She has taught as an adjunct professor at Georgetown University and the University of Maryland. In spring 2008, she spent three months on General David Petraeus's (Ret.) staff in Baghdad. Cragin also has conducted fieldwork in Pakistan, Yemen, Egypt, northwest China, Indonesia, the Philippines, and Sri Lanka, among others. She is the author of *Women as Terrorists: Mothers, Recruiters, and Martyrs* (Praeger, 2009), and her RAND publications include a contribution to *The Long Shadow of 9/11: America's Response to Terrorism*; *Social Science for Counterterrorism*; and *Sharing the Dragon's Teeth: Terrorist Groups and the Exchange of New Technologies*. Cragin also has published in such journals as *Terrorism and Political Violence*, *Studies in Conflict and Terrorism*, and the *Historical Journal*.

(U) William Giannetti is a Senior Intelligence Analyst from DIA. His 18-year career spans time as a civil servant, Philadelphia cop and military intelligence officer. He served two tours in Afghanistan and has a M.A. in Criminal Justice from St. Joseph's University.

(U) Barbara A. Grewe is a Principal Policy Advisor for the MITRE Corporation where she serves as a trusted advisor to senior government leaders and has been responsible for leading interagency efforts to address high priority issues. She previously served as a Senior Counsel on the 9/11 Commission where she was responsible for investigating several key areas. She has also served as an Associate General Counsel in the Government Accountability Office and as an Assistant United States Attorney for the District of Columbia. She has a J.D. from the University of Michigan Law School, an M.A. (Oxon.) from the University of Oxford (where she was a Rhodes Scholar), and a B.A. from Wellesley College.

(U) Christine "Chris" Healey served as the top legal advisor to the Senate Select Committee on Intelligence. She worked for the Government Affairs Committee on the landmark legislation that reformed the intelligence community and created the position of the Director of National Intelligence. Healey also served as a Senior Counsel and team leader on the 9/11 Commission. Prior to that, she was on the House Permanent Select Committee on Intelligence, including as staff director.

(U) Seth G. Jones is director of the International Security and Defense Policy Center at the RAND Corporation, as well as an adjunct professor at Johns Hopkins University's School for Advanced International Studies (SAIS). He served in numerous positions in US Special Operations Command, including as an advisor to the commanding general in Afghanistan. He is the author of *Hunting in the Shadows: The Pursuit of al Qa'ida after 9/11* (W.W. Norton, 2012), and received his M.A. and Ph.D. from the University of Chicago.

(U) Johanna Keena is a Staff Operations Specialist for the FBI focusing on counterterrorism. She previously served at a legal and lobbying firm. Keena has received an M.S. in Intelligence Management from the University of Maryland University College.

(U) Joseph Moreno is a former federal prosecutor with the United States Department of Justice in the National Security Division. Currently a Major in the United States Army Reserve Judge Advocate General Corps, Joseph is a two-time combat veteran of Operations Iraqi Freedom and Enduring Freedom, and recipient of the Bronze Star Medal for his service in Iraq. He currently works in private practice at the law firm Cadwalader, Wickersham & Taft LLP in Washington DC. Moreno has a B.A. from Stony Brook University, a J.D./M.B.A. from St. John's University, and is a certified public accountant.

(U) Jamie Pirko is a Security and Intelligence Analyst, in the area of National Security for US government agencies including the DOD, FBI, and the Congressional Commission on the Prevention of Weapons of Mass Destruction. Before joining the Commission, she served as an Intelligence Analyst in the FBI's Weapons of Mass Destruction Domain Awareness program.

(U) Elisabeth Poteat is an attorney with the National Security Division's Counterterrorism Section in US Department of Justice, where she has served on the National Security Cyber Specialists Network and the Antiterrorism Advisory Council. She is a former organized crime prosecutor at the US Attorney's Office for Washington, D.C., and a former Deputy Public Defender for Los Angeles. She is the author of two recent works on classified information: "Discovering the Artichoke: How Omissions Have Blurred the Enabling Intent of the Classified Information Procedures Act" (*Journal of National Security Law and Policy Vol. 7*); and a chapter, "How Classified Information is Handled in Leak Cases," in the book *Whistleblowers, Leaks, and the Media: The First Amendment and National Security,* ABA, 2014.

(U) William Richardson served 32 years at CIA, where he held numerous senior leadership positions in the Directorate of Intelligence at CIA Headquarters and overseas. He also served as the DNI's National Intelligence Manager for South Asia, and as the intelligence briefer to President Barack Obama and Vice President Al Gore.

(U) Amy Buenning Sturm is an analyst for US Special Operations Command and has eight years of government and non-profit experience focused on counterterrorism and national security issues. She is a Ph.D. student at University of Maryland's School of Public Policy and earned an M.A. in Security Studies from Georgetown University in 2010. Sturm is a Truman Scholar and a former Herbert Scoville Jr. Peace Fellow.

(U) Caryn Wagner is a former Under Secretary of Intelligence and Analysis at the Department of Homeland Security. Prior to that, she was a 30-year intelligence professional who began her career as a Signals Intelligence officer in the United States Army. Wagner spent seven years at DIA, where she served as the Deputy Director for Analysis and Production, and on the staff of the House Permanent Select Committee on Intelligence, and as Budget Director. She also served as Director of the IC Community Management Staff, the Assistant Deputy Director of National Intelligence for Management, and as first Chief Financial Officer for the National Intelligence Program.

CHAPTER I
(U) BASELINE: THE FBI TODAY

(U) The mandate of the FBI 9/11 Review Commission, (hereafter Review Commission) is to measure the Bureau's progress over "yesterdays" since 9/11 and to assess its preparedness for "tomorrows" in a rapidly evolving and dangerous world. To accomplish this, the Review Commission worked to determine how close the Bureau is today to its goal of becoming a threat-based, intelligence-driven organization, and to ascertain the extent to which this complies with the 9/11 Commission's recommendation that the Bureau transform itself into America's premier domestic intelligence agency. The report also looks ahead to an evolving and increasingly complex threat environment that should drive reform in the Bureau.

(U) This first chapter will provide background and perspective on the Review Commission's findings developed in the following chapters, a broader look at relevant national and global trends that have driven FBI reforms in recent years, a summary of the related initiatives put forth by former Director Robert S. Mueller, III, and a description of where the Review Commission sees the Bureau's transformation today—its 2015 baseline.

(U) Key Points

- (U) The FBI has made measurable progress over the past decade in developing end-to-end intelligence capabilities and in significantly improving information sharing and collaboration with key partners at home and abroad. This has undoubtedly contributed to protecting the Homeland against another catastrophic terrorist attack. But progress in building key intelligence programs, analysis and Human Intelligence (HUMINT) collection in particular, lag behind marked advances in law enforcement capabilities. This imbalance needs urgently to be addressed to meet growing and increasingly complex national security threats, including from adaptive and increasingly tech-savvy terrorists, more brazen computer hackers, and more technically capable, global cyber syndicates.

- (U) The FBI's reform efforts have been impeded—but never halted—by early confusion with regard to the Department of Justice (DOJ) and Director of National Intelligence (DNI) guidance on intelligence activities, by the uneven commitment of mid-level leadership to intelligence-focused transformation, by a one-year budget process out of sync with the five-year cycle of the major intelligence agencies, by an initial cultural clash between seasoned special agents and a vastly expanded cadre of inexperienced analysts, by conflicting structural recommendations from the 9/11 and weapons of mass destruction (WMD) commissions, and by the negative impact of sequestration on multiple reform initiatives.

- (U) The FBI requires a five-year, top-down strategic plan to provide the resources needed to upgrade its support services—including information technology (IT), procurement, contracting, and security—and to achieve its growing mission as a global, intelligence-driven investigative service. The plan must enable the professionalization of FBI analysis, the improvement of HUMINT capabilities, a more focused and long-term attention to the Legal Attachés (LEGAT) program, the recognition of science and technology (S&T) as a core competency for future investment, and closer relations with Congressional committees of jurisdiction to ensure that the Bureau has both the state-of the art capabilities to counter increasingly dangerous threats and the effective internal safeguards to protect civil liberties.

(U) The full report, which is based on 10 months of formal internal briefings and research, extensive outside interviews, and 14 field visits, concludes that the Bureau has made important progress in building a "specialized and integrated national security work force" yet must accelerate its efforts and deepen progress in several critical areas.[10] Director Mueller pursued this goal relentlessly for a dozen years, by centralizing key functions in a field-dominated bureaucracy, launching multiple programs and processes to build an end-to-end intelligence process within the FBI, and significantly improving collaboration and information sharing with partners at home and abroad. A list of select intelligence program developments can be found in Appendix C. These changes, consistently implemented year-after-year, demonstrate the Bureau's commitment to its national security and intelligence program reform. The Review Commission evaluated several of these reform efforts, many of which were well intentioned but fell short in execution, with an eye toward recommendations for the future.

(U) The Review Commission also responded to the Congressional mandate to identify obstacles to reform efforts. Director Mueller's initiatives were impeded by the early institutional struggle to reconcile the Domestic Investigations and Operations Guide (DIOG) and the (DNI) guidance on intelligence activities, the initial cultural clash between special agents and a suddenly vastly expanded cadre of new analysts, conflicting structural recommendations from the 9/11 and WMD commissions, and the severe impact of sequestration on multiple reform initiatives. Progress also was hindered by the uneven commitment to reform of FBI leadership in the field. The Bureau's efforts to integrate its intelligence and law enforcement missions continue to be constrained by a bifurcated annual budget process—versus five-year cycles of other intelligence agencies—that runs through the rigorous review of separate DOJ and Office of the Director of National Intelligence (ODNI) budget offices and on to Congressional committees of jurisdiction, which are similarly divided between intelligence and law enforcement priorities. This lack of alignment between Executive and Legislative overseers needs to be addressed as the Bureau develops a multi-year strategic plan. The Review Commission took all this into account in assessing the Bureau's progress.

(U) The Bureau's goal for intelligence during the Mueller era, which is consistent with the basic recommendation of the 9/11 Commission, was stated in the FBI Strategic Plan, 2004-2009: "The FBI has a mandate from the President, Congress, the Attorney General, and the DCI (Director of Central Intelligence) to protect national security by producing intelligence in support of its own investigative mission, national intelligence priorities, and the needs of other customers."[11] The Review Commission has taken the Director's commitment to these three customer sets as the standard for testing the Bureau's performance today.

(U) The Urgency of the Threat

(U) The Review Commission recognizes that national security threats to the United States have multiplied, and become increasingly complex and more globally dispersed in the past decade. Hostile states and transnational networks—including cyber hackers and organized syndicates, space-system intruders, WMD proliferators, narcotics and human traffickers, and other organized

---

10 (U) *The 9/11 Commission Report*, 425.
11 (U) Federal Bureau of Investigation, *FBI Strategic Plan, 2004-2009* (2003): 20.

16

criminals—are operating against American interests across national borders, and within the United States. In the coming decade, these evolving threats will increasingly challenge the FBI's leadership at every level, its traditional culture, and all of its core capabilities in criminal investigation, counterintelligence, intelligence collection and analysis, and technology. The extensive reforms of the past decade must be accelerated to fulfill the Bureau's expanded global mission as a fully integrated, intelligence-driven investigative organization.

(U) Decentralized terrorist networks and militias— so evident today in the Middle East, sub-Saharan Africa, and South Asia—are recruiting homegrown violent extremists from Western countries to their fights that are suffused in jihadist rhetoric but also fueled by the growing instability and widening violence of failing states. These foreign fighters, including growing numbers of US citizens, are a clear and present security threat to the United States due to their training and experience on the jihadist battlefield and to the prospect of their return to the United States and other countries. Extremists, who are now inspired through social media and recruited on the internet, increasingly pose a domestic threat given the propaganda and encouragement emanating from overseas to carry out attacks at home.

(U) All of these state and non-state adversaries of the United States are becoming more adaptive and sophisticated in their strategies, more advanced in their use of technology, and more successful in their counterintelligence operations. They are exploiting rapid advances in IT, including sophisticated use of social media, to accelerate the real-time flow of their operational information (including bomb-making expertise), and of their people, finances, and transfers of weapons across borders. The continuing broader IT-driven revolution in dual-use technologies—including biotechnology, nanotechnology, material sciences, neuroscience, and robotics—challenges the FBI to understand how these technologies, separately and in synergistic combination, outpace its own current tradecraft and strengthen that of its adversaries.

(U) What is the Goal?

(U) The Review Commission based its findings and recommendations on its vision of what a fully operational threat-based, intelligence-driven FBI would look like. The FBI, as the core of US domestic intelligence, can never be identical to the Central Intelligence Agency (CIA) or any other national intelligence agency. Criminal investigators openly pursue and handle evidence under strong internal and external constraints—including the US Constitution and generations of law aimed at protecting civil liberties. In contrast, intelligence officers in national agencies pursue information abroad in secret with fewer of these constraints and with an abundance of incentives to assess risk and probability virtually unconstrained.

(U) A Model for US Domestic Intelligence

(U) The Review Commission's vision of the future FBI is one in which criminal investigation, counterintelligence, intelligence collection and analysis, and science and technology applications are seen as complementary core competencies of a global intelligence and investigative organization. These competencies are applied to the same criminal and national security missions, and intersect synergistically in mission support—with a budget that incentivizes the integration. But these competencies remain as distinct professional disciplines requiring their own investment strategies, specialized training, and discipline-managed career services. The FBI will fulfill its domestic intelligence role with analysts and collectors who are grounded in criminal investigation; who have ready access to state-of-the-art technology; who continuously exploit the systems, tools, and relationships of the national intelligence agencies; and who both cultivate and benefit from robust Continental United States (CONUS) and outside the Continental United States (OCONUS) collaborative relationships that widen the Bureau's access to both investigative leads and reportable intelligence. Achieving this should not be a zero-sum game between intelligence analysis and investigation. It should mean a continued FBI commitment to a growing criminal investigation mission, a tighter and smoother integration of intelligence analysts and collectors into the USIC, and increasingly closer collaborative relationships with US and foreign partners. US domestic intelligence, with the FBI at its hub, will be a collaborative enterprise optimizing the integration of international, federal, state, local, and community players.

(U) Enduring Drivers of Reform

(U) The FBI has been slow to adapt at times in its 106-year history, but it has never stood still. Its progression has not been linear. Some eras were more challenging than others, some responses were bolder, and some lapses—including the covert and frequently illegal Counterintelligence Program (COINTELPRO) that peaked in the 1960s—blemished the record. But the Bureau's success against a wide range of targets over the years has been impressive by any reckoning. Its targets for investigation have included WWI-era anarchists, notorious bank robbers in the post-WWI decades, Prohibition-era gangsters, Nazi saboteurs, Soviet spies, illegal drug traffickers, violent militias, white supremacists, Ku Klux Klan "dragons," air-land-and-sea hijackers, legions of corrupt politicians, domestic and foreign organized crime bosses, human traffickers, weapons proliferators, child pornographers, crooked corporate executives, identity thieves, cyber criminals, and both domestic and international terrorists. And from the beginning, the Bureau has always supported its law enforcement mission by collecting and analyzing intelligence.

(U) For the past several decades, however, the Bureau's job has gotten much harder as increasingly complex threats have demanded unprecedented intelligence support and analytic capability in the midst of a global information revolution. For this more focused intelligence mission, it is still a work in progress. Since the early 1980s, three intersecting trends have pushed the FBI to change the way it does business. First, the Cold War world order has been transformed by the collapse of the Soviet Union and by nuclear Russia's troubling response to its loss of global stature, the dramatic rise of China, and the emergence of multi-polar regional powers in the European Union, Brazil, Mexico, Iran, South Korea, and India. Regional instability has grown with the proliferation of new terrorist organizations unaffiliated with nation states, insurgent groups, and countless violence-prone militias that flow across defenseless borders of failing states in the Middle East, Africa, and South Asia. America now exists in a world of globally distributed threats, and this complicated picture will only expand and become more complex in the decades ahead.

(U) The second trend involves the rapid pace of technology research and development (R&D), which is now a challenging global phenomenon that was once wholly dominated by the United States. According to the National Academies of Science, China— with 1.3 billion people— today has the capacity for technological innovation, as does the tiny island nation of Singapore (5.5 million people) in the Malaccan Straits, along with several Western countries.[12] Foreign R&D continues to make rapid advances in key areas such as IT, biotechnology, DNA applications, nanotechnology, material sciences, neuroscience, and robotics—all with worrisome dual-use implications.

(U) IT-driven globalization has led individuals, nations, non-government organizations, and multi-national corporations to leverage international networks for the good of mankind. At the same time, terrorists, organized criminals, and other state and non-state actors hostile to the United States are able to move people, ideological information, finance, and catastrophic destructive know-how across borders in real time with unprecedented ease. Al-Qa'ida exploited global networks—below the radar of Western intelligence agencies—to plan and execute the 9/11 attacks. Homegrown jihadists in Madrid and London, connected to al-Qa'ida terrorists, carried out catastrophic attacks against urban transportation in 2004 and 2005. Today, a proliferation of terrorist groups—including the formidable Islamic State of Iraq and the Levant (ISIL)—and militias in the Middle East and sub-Saharan Africa are exploiting social media with increasing sophistication and effectiveness.

(U) The internet gave Usama bin Laden a global platform to energize and expand his jihadist following. It also gave rise to other charismatic leaders like the infamous US-born cleric, Anwar al-Aulaqi, who effectively exploited the internet to recruit young Islamic extremists, including his fellow Americans, and to lead them to jihadist violence. A growing number of US citizens or permanent residents—Jose Padilla, Najibullah Zazi, David Coleman Headley, Faisal Shahzad, Nidal Hasan, and Boston Marathon bombers Tamerlan and Dzhokar Tsarnaev, were radicalized, in part, via the internet and/or emboldened by jihadist training and/or contacts abroad. So was 22-year-old Moner Mohammad Abusallah, an impressionable Florida-raised basketball fan, who succesfully traveled to and from Syria and died a suicide bomber there in May 2014, while avoiding disruption by western intelligence agencies.

(U) The third trend concerns the growing US demand in recent years for a more capable domestic intelligence service. This results from the unprecedented intersection of adverse geopolitics and advancing technology since the 1980s, punctuated by the national trauma of the 9/11 terrorist attacks. Americans were understandably rattled by the "backyard" proximity of the al-Qa'ida terrorist threat. Not surprisingly, new national security stakeholders emerged at the

---

12 (U) The National Research Council of the National Academies, *S&T Strategies of Six Countries: Implications for the United States* (Washington, D.C., The National Academies Press, 2010): 81-91.

state and local levels, including first-responders who claimed a legitimate need for intelligence support from the Federal Government and a collaborative hand from the FBI. First responders today have been encouraged, for good reason, to see the Bureau as the core of US domestic intelligence. Many say that it could do a better job keeping them informed.

(U) Relevant Pre-9/11 Reforms

(U) The USIC, the police community, and Congress responded to this new, distributed threat environment in the mid-1980s, with the pace picking up dramatically in the ensuing decade. A brief synopsis of the period reveals two critical facts to be gleaned about the FBI's reformist efforts. First, the FBI leadership had impressive insight into its challenges before 9/11 and developed a visionary strategic plan in the late 1990s to address them. Second, it did not implement its own well-crafted plan to change the way it was doing business in the face of a growing terrorist threat. Anecdotal testimony indicates that the plan lost momentum for a variety of reasons, including competing pressures on leadership, DOJ reluctance to buy into the growing counterterrorism mission, the inattention of Congressional oversight, and the inherent difficulty of moving a field office-dominated bureaucracy. Whatever the cause of the plan's demise, the lesson of history is that the FBI and the United States would have been well served by its implementation.

(U) The FBI supported United States Intelligence Community (USIC) reforms and participated in many joint efforts. In 1982, Director William H. Webster, in response to an upsurge in global terrorist attacks, made counterterrorism a fourth Bureau priority. In 1984, the Hostage Taking Act (18 U.S.C. §1203) extended FBI jurisdiction to investigate terrorist acts against US citizens abroad. In 1986, Congress passed the Omnibus Diplomatic Security and Antiterrorism Act (HR-4418), which established a new extraterritorial statute related to terrorist acts against US citizens or interests abroad. The DCI stood up the Counterterrorism Center (CTC) at CIA in 1986, integrating FBI agents, followed by the Counternarcotics Center and several iterations of a counter-proliferation center—all mandated to promote interagency rotations, to focus collection, to integrate analysis, and to promote information sharing. Both CIA and the Defense Intelligence Agency (DIA) reorganized their intelligence units in the mid-1990s to meet new threats and to enable technology. The FBI took similar steps later in the decade, including stepping up its collaborative dialogue and leadership exchanges with the CIA. The White House in 1998 established the position of National Coordinator for Security, Infrastructure Protection, and Counterterrorism.

(U) In 1989, DOJ authorized the Bureau to arrest terrorist suspects without the consent of their country of residence. The FBI launched a new counterterrorism division in 1999. The FBI, along with other USIC components, introduced commendable reform initiatives in the 1990s, though they did not all take hold. Every CIA directorate, along with many counterparts in other agencies, developed strategic plans and multiple reorganizations in the 1990s. Advancing technology drove the controversial creation of the National Imagery and Mapping Agency (NIMA) in 1996. NIMA (later named National Geospatial-Intelligence Agency-NGA) launched a major push to get ahead of the geospatial technology curve, while the National Security Agency (NSA) began a fundamental transformation to adapt to the global revolution in communications technology. In 1998, the Ballistic Missile Commission, headed by Donald Rumsfeld, included with its report a side letter critiquing USIC analytic performance that was an impressive blueprint for reform. The FBI significantly increased its overseas LEGAT presence and developed a five-year strategic plan in the late 1990s that included goals to develop a comprehensive global intelligence collection and analytic capability.

(U) The Bureau issued the *FBI Strategic Plan, 1998-2003: Keeping Tomorrow Safe* in May 1998. The plan, seven months in the making under the leadership of Deputy Director Robert "Bear" Bryant, included the strategic goal to "prevent, disrupt, and defeat terrorist operations before they occur."[13] It pointed to the imperative for the Bureau to boost its performance in intelligence collection and analysis, threat prioritization, S&T, IT systems and applications, and in collaboration with other United States government (USG) agencies and with state and local partners. It also upgraded multiple management and business processes essential to implementing the plan.

(U) The FBI leadership in the era of Director Louis J. Freeh experienced an intelligence world turning upside down and was closely involved in the establishment of the USIC centers. DCI William Webster went from the FBI to CIA in 1987 committed to a counterterrorism mission that was growing rapidly along with international organized crime—including the Sicilian mafia operating in the United States. In December 1988, Libyan terrorists blew up Pan Am 103 over Lockerbie, Scotland, killing 270 people, and raising the investigative profile of both the FBI and a leading DOJ official, Robert Mueller. In June 1996, Saudi Hizballah bombed Khobar Towers, a US military residence in Dharan, Saudi Arabia, killing 19. An FBI investigation ensued, led by then Assistant United States Attorney James Comey.

(U) In this unsettling period, the FBI and the USIC generally increased their appreciation for analysis to help guide collection and to focus operations against complex global threats. In 2000, the new FBI Executive Assistant Director (EAD) for Counterterrorism, Dale Watson, produced a prescient strategic plan called MAXCAP05, which sought sensibly to build intelligence and analysis capacity against the terrorist threat over the next five years. The FBI also participated with USIC analytic units in the work of the Community-wide National Intelligence Producers Board (NIPB), which did a baseline assessment of USIC analytic capabilities and followed it up early in 2001 with a strategic investment plan for community analysis.[14] The FBI was emphasizing a stronger attention to counterterrorism and a greater reliance on intelligence long before 9/11.

(U) The investment plan flagged to Congress the alarming decline in investment in analysis across the USIC and the urgent need to build or strengthen interagency training, database interoperability, collaborative networks, a system for threat prioritization, links to outside experts, and an effective open-source strategy. A strong consensus, which included the FBI,

---

13 (U) Federal Bureau of Investigation, *FBI Strategic Plan 1998-2003: Keeping Tomorrow Safe* (1998): 12.
14 (U) Central Intelligence Agency, *Strategic Investment Plan for Intelligence Community Analysis* (2000-2001): 7-76. Special agent Steven McCraw, who represented the FBI on the NIPB, became the Assistant Director of the Office of Intelligence and Inspections under the first Executive Assistant Director of Intelligence, Maureen Baginski, prior to his retirement in 2004.

concluded that the USIC needed to transform, and it was transforming but not fast enough to counter the growing threat from the flat, agile, global network of al-Qa'ida.

(U) The principal lesson learned from this brief history of USIC and FBI reform is that the Bureau has talented and dedicated leaders capable of identifying and addressing its weaknesses and of laying out a clear multi-year plan to do so.

(U) Baseline 2004

(U) In its report published in July 2004, the 9/11 Commission found there were significant inadequacies in the capabilities and management of the FBI, in particular with respect to its domestic intelligence mission and its role within the USIC, that had contributed to the USG's failure in preventing the 9/11 attacks.[15] The 9/11 Commission found that before the attacks the FBI favored its traditional criminal justice mission over its national security mission. While the 9/11 Commission noted that the FBI "maintained an active counterintelligence function and was the lead agency for the investigation of foreign terrorist groups operating within the United States," the 9/11 Commission did not believe the FBI's analytical and preventative efforts were as strong as the criminal investigative abilities it was able to bring to bear after terrorist attacks occurred, such as with the 1993 World Trade Center bombing, the 1998 East Africa embassy bombings, and the attack on the USS Cole in Yemen in 2000.

(U) In view of the intelligence and security failures it found at the FBI and across the USG, the 9/11 Commission considered, but explicitly rejected, recommending the creation of a completely new domestic intelligence agency, separate and apart from the FBI—generally referred to as the British MI5 (also known as the British Security Service or BSS) model for an internal security service. The Review Commission strongly agrees with the 9/11 Commission's judgment that there were many factors against creating a new agency, first among them that the FBI was already "accustomed to carrying out sensitive intelligence collection operations in compliance with the law."[16] Instead, the 9/11 Commission saw a reformed FBI playing a "vital" role within the context of the 9/11 Commission's full set of recommendations for structural changes to the USIC. These were intended to organize and equip the Federal Government, and the USIC in particular, to conduct joint operational planning and joint analysis, "not just for countering terrorism, but for the broader range of national security challenges in the decades ahead."[17]
(U) While the 9/11 Commission applauded what it described as "significant progress" that had already been made under Director Mueller since the attacks to improve intelligence capabilities

---

15 (U) *The 9/11 Commission Report,* 352.
16 (U) *The 9/11 Commission Report,* 423. In addition, the Commission concluded the FBI benefited from the oversight it received as a component of the Department of Justice; creation of a new agency would divert the attention of high-level officials while the threat of terrorism remained high; any new agency would require a range of assets and personnel already present within the FBI; and with both intelligence and law enforcement authorities, revised by the USA PATRIOT Act, within one agency there were new opportunities for cooperative action as counterterrorism investigations quickly become matters that result in criminal prosecutions.
17 (U) *The 9/11 Commission Report,* 407, 423. These recommendations, among others, for counterterrorism, were "to create a strong national intelligence center, part of [the National Counterterrorist Center (NCTC)], that will oversee counterterrorism intelligence work, foreign and domestic, and to create a National Intelligence Director "who can set and enforce standards for the collection, processing and reporting of information."

within the Bureau, the 9/11 Commission worried that the FBI might ultimately fall short in reforming and restructuring itself to address the transnational issues faced by the United States.[18] In particular, the 9/11 Commission found "gaps between some of the announced reforms and the reality in the field," fearing that at some point the system could "revert to a focus on lower-priority criminal justice cases over national security requirements."[19] The current Review Commission has found this concern to be justified.

(U) Emphasizing the need for the FBI to "make an all-out effort to institutionalize change," particularly in its field offices, the 9/11 Commission recommended that the Bureau establish "a specialized and integrated national security workforce. . . consisting of agents, analysts, linguists, and surveillance specialists who are recruited, trained, rewarded, and retained to ensure the development of an institutional culture imbued with a deep expertise in intelligence and national security."[20] The 9/11 Commission recommended the creation of a culture where "FBI agents and analysts in the field [would] have sustained support and dedicated resources to become stronger intelligence officers." The 9/11 Commission also recommended that agents and analysts be brought into the Bureau with appropriate educational and professional backgrounds and work together with linguists and surveillance personnel in the field so that "a dedicated team approach is brought to bear on national security intelligence operations."[21]

(U) As the 9/11 Commission noted, the FBI had already embarked on internal reforms prior to the issuance of the 9/11 Commission report.[22] The FBI was operating under new counterterrorism authorities, with new resources, provided by Congress in the immediate aftermath of the attacks.[23] New entities had been created to improve intelligence analysis and respond to terrorism threats. At the most senior level, the FBI Director began to work closely on a daily basis with the DCI and other officials in the USIC to brief the President and address threats.[24]

(U) Progress in the Mueller Era

(U) The Review Commission reviewed multiple initiatives under Director Mueller to build an intelligence collection and analysis capability. Some programs fared better than others, and several needed deeper implementation along the way. The Bureau under Director Mueller was required to respond to inconsistent structural recommendations from successive commissions, disruption from the rapid infusion of minimally trained analysts, "reorganization fatigue" from repeated efforts to hit the target, and the devastating impact of sequestration to its transformation

---

18 (U) *The 9/11 Commission Report,* 425.

19 (U) Ibid., 425.

20 (U) Ibid.

21 (U) *The 9/11 Commission Report,* 426.

22 (U) Federal Bureau of Investigation, *Report to the National Commission on Terrorist Attacks upon the United States: The FBI's Counterterrorism Program Since September 2001,* 2004, http://www.fbi.gov/stats-services/publications/fbi_ct_911com_0404.pdf (accessed on December 11, 2014): 1-3.

23 (U) Jerome P. Bjelopera, *The Federal Bureau of Investigation and Terrorism Investigations (FBI Terrorism Investigations)* (Congressional Research Service, April 24, 2013): 2-9.

24 (U) Garrett M. Graff, *The Threat Matrix* (The Threat Matrix) (New York: Little, Brown and Company, 2011): 17-19.

efforts. All this notwithstanding, the Review Commission has observed a continued strong commitment in the Bureau to build the intelligence capacity that Mueller initiated.

(U) By the time the 9/11 Commission issued its report on July 22, 2004, Director Mueller had announced a new list of the Bureau's 10 priorities, with "protect the United States from terrorist attack" at the top.[25] In immediate response to the 9/11 attacks, most of the FBI's 11,000 special agents and thousands of additional personnel were transferred to the PENTTBOM investigation.[26] After the initial response, the FBI reprioritized its efforts, particularly with respect to traditional law enforcement activities that could be handled by other federal, state or local law enforcement agencies. On a permanent basis, by FY05, the number of authorized counterterrorism personnel had doubled from FY2000 levels.[27] In October 2001 Director Mueller ordered the creation of Joint Terrorism Task Forces (JTTFs), in every field office.[28] Expansion of the JTTFs was coupled with additional efforts to work with state and municipal law enforcement.[29] Specialized counterterrorism entities, such as the terrorism financing operations section and the document exploitation unit, were created or expanded both within the FBI and as collaborative, multi-agency task forces.[30]

(U) The FBI also took a number of steps before the 9/11 Commission issued its report to improve its intelligence mission and the integration of intelligence into its investigations. An Office of Intelligence was created separate from operational divisions at the end of 2001. Intelligence training was expanded for agents and analysts and intelligence reporting increased dramatically.[31] In recognition of the connection of the terrorist threat with other criminal activity, the intelligence effort was extended across all FBI programs and was headed by an EAD for Intelligence, Maureen Baginski, an accomplished regional analyst with extensive experience in technical collection, from NSA. In October 2003, under Baginski's leadership, Field Intelligence Groups (FIGs) were established in every field office to coordinate, manage, and conduct FBI intelligence functions in the field.[32] Intelligence was seen, at least by FBI Headquarters, as the mechanism by which the FBI would become threat-driven versus case-driven and integrated into the larger USIC's requirements. The FIGs responded directly to a core recommendation of the 9/11 Commission.

---

25 (U) *FBI Terrorism Investigations,* 5. The other nine priorities were: protect the United States against foreign intelligence operations and espionage; protect the United States against cyber-based attacks and high-technology crimes; combat public corruption at all levels; protect civil rights; combat transnational and national criminal organizations and enterprises; combat major white-collar crime; combat significant violent crime; support federal, state, municipal and international partners; and upgrade technology to successfully perform the FBI's mission.

26 (U) PENTTBOM was the name given to the FBI's investigation into the 9/11 attacks. Its name is derived from the fact that the attacks took place at the Pentagon, in Pennsylvania, and at the Twin Towers.

27 (U) *FBI Terrorism Investigations,* 7.

28 (U) As of 2014, there were 103 JTTFs (71 created after 9/11), as well as the National Joint Terrorism Task Force (NJTTF) and the Foreign Terrorist Tracking Task Force (FTTTF).

29 (U) *FBI Terrorism Investigations,* 37-39.

30 (U) The NJTTF, FTTTF, and Special Technologies and Applications Section (STAS), for example, were created in 2002. The creation of the Terrorist Threat Integration Center, a multi-agency organization primarily including CIA, FBI, and DHS personnel, was announced in January 2003.

31 (U) Federal Bureau of Investigation Training Division Briefing, *Integrated Curriculum Initiative,* June 26, 2014: 1-2.

32 (U) *FBI Terrorism Investigations,* 28.

(U) The FBI also reported to the 9/11 Commission that it was making substantial progress upgrading its information technology and re-engineering its administrative processes, both to modernize, and streamline its operations and to improve the recruiting, training and leadership development of its personnel.[33]

(U) Many of the FBI's new authorities were contained in the USA PATRIOT Act of 2001, enacted in October 2001.[34] The USA PATRIOT Act amended several existing statutes, such as the Foreign Intelligence Surveillance Act of 1978 (50 U.S.C. §1801 *et. seq*), the Electronic Communications Privacy Act of 1986 (47 U.S.C. §§ 1001-1010), and the laws governing the issuance of National Security Letters (NSLs) (12 U.S.C. § 3414(a)(5)(A); 15 U.S.C.§§ 1681u and 1681v; 18 U.S.C. § 2709, and; 50 U.S.C. § 436) , facilitating the collection of information relevant for authorized international terrorism investigations. Importantly, the Act broke down the perceived wall that had impeded the sharing of information between intelligence and criminal investigators. Director Mueller later testified to Congress that "the USA PATRIOT Act has changed the way the FBI operates. Many of our counterterrorism successes are the direct result of the provisions of the Act."[35]

(U) The FBI also centralized command and control of counterterrorism operations at Headquarters.[36] This was a significant departure from past practice at the FBI and not without controversy. Special Agent in Charge (SACs) of field offices no longer had sole control of their counterterrorism cases and did not have the authority to adjust resources within their offices away from the national counterterrorism priority.[37] Every terrorism lead was to be investigated with results reported back to Headquarters.[38] While some agents and the counterterrorism squads in the New York Field Office, in particular, had been conducting sophisticated investigations to map their multi-jurisdictional and international targets, develop intelligence, and disrupt ongoing activities, the FBI did not have the policies and protocols to realize the benefits of intelligence analysis of this kind within the Bureau as a whole or with other intelligence agency partners.[39] The FBI's information technology was inadequate to support intelligence analysis within a case, and the FBI lacked the mechanisms to allow for the information sharing necessary to support intelligence analysis on a broader basis.[40]

---

33 (U) Ibid., 51-62. FBI's assessment of its Virtual Case File (VCF) was optimistic, though the system had inherent flaws. VCF was eventually scrapped after $170 million was spent and eventually replaced by Sentinel in 2005. Sentinel, an information and investigative case management system, was not finally made available to all FBI employees until July 1, 2012. The Department of Justice Inspector General has completed ten interim audits of Sentinel. See US Department of Justice, Office of the Inspector General, *Audit of the Status of the Federal Bureau of Investigation's Sentinel Program*, Audit Report 14-31, September, 2014, https://www.justice.gov/oig/reports/2014/a1431.pdf (accessed on December 11, 2014): 1.

34 (U) Uniting and Strengthening America by Providing Appropriate Tools Required to Intercept and Obstruct Terrorism Act of 2001 (USA PATRIOT Act), P.L. 107-56.

35 (U) *FBI Investigations*, 9 (citing U.S. Congress, Senate Committee on the Judiciary, *Sunset Provisions of the USA Patriot Act*, Testimony of Robert Mueller, Director, FBI, 109th Cong., 1st Sess., April 5, 2005.)

36 (U) FBI briefing, *The Evolution of the National Security Branch*, January 2014.

37 (U) *FBI Terrorism Investigations*, 11.

38 (U) Ibid.

39 (U) *The Threat Matrix*, 425.

40 (U) *FBI Terrorism Investigations*, 51-56.

(U) International activities, which had grown under Director Freeh's tenure with the opening of 21 additional LEGAT offices and the temporary deployment of hundreds of agents overseas for investigations such as the East African embassy and USS Cole bombings, further intensified.[41] The FBI sent teams of agents, analysts, and other professionals to Kuwait and Iraq starting before the March 2003 beginning of the second Gulf War to work cooperatively with the US military and other government agencies on the exploitation of Iraqi Government documents and investigations of improvised explosive devices, among other duties. An Arabic-speaking FBI agent was the team leader responsible for the seven-month interrogation of Saddam Hussein after his capture in December 2003.[42]

(U) Following the publication of the 9/11 Commission report, the FBI continued to evolve both as a result of internal and external reviews and in response to the direction of the President and Congress. Congress passed the Intelligence Reform and Terrorism Prevention Act of 2004 (IRTPA) to enact the recommendations made by the 9/11 Commission.[43] The second of the Act's eight titles was devoted to the Federal Bureau of Investigation and directed the President to establish a Directorate of Intelligence (DI) and maintain an intelligence career service within the FBI. By a memorandum to the Attorney General, dated November 16, 2004, the President had already directed the FBI to create a DI.

(U) Even as Congress was setting forth in legislation the majority of the recommendations of the 9/11 Commission, a presidential commission was investigating the pre-war judgments of the USIC with respect to the presence of WMD within Iraq.[44] During its tenure, the WMD Commission was asked by President George W. Bush to make recommendations regarding how IRTPA should be implemented.

(U) Although the WMD Commission found the FBI has "made significant strides in creating an effective intelligence capability," it nonetheless mandated far-reaching changes in the organization and management of intelligence.[45] In a letter to President Bush on March 29, 2005, the WMD Commission argued that the establishment of the DI was insufficient to create a "specialized and integrated national security workforce" because it did not provide the EAD for the DI with authority for "vertically integrating foreign intelligence collection, analysis, and

---

41 (U) *FBI Terrorism Investigations,* 46. As of December 2014, there are 64 FBI LEGAT offices around the world.
42 (U) The team consisted of CIA analysts and FBI agents, intelligence analysts, language specialists and a behavioral profiler. *Interviewing Saddam: FBI Agent Gets to the Truth,* http://www.fbi.gov/news/stories/2008/january/piro012808 (accessed on January 9, 2015); *The Threat Matrix,* 456 – 463. George Piro later served as head of the High-Value Detainee Interrogation Group from 2011-2013.
43 (U) Intelligence Reform and Terrorism Prevention Act of 2004, P.L. 108-458 (December 17, 2004).
44 (U) Later legislation on implementing the recommendations of the 9/11 Commission was enacted as well. See Implementing the Recommendations of the 9/11 Commission Act of 2007 P.L. 110-53 (August 3, 2007). See also http://www.dhs.gov/xlibrary/assets/implementing-9-11-commission-report-progress-2011.pdf; http://www.gpo.gov/fdsys/pkg/PLAW-110publ53/content-detail.html; https://www.nsa.gov/civil_liberties/_files/pl_110_53_sec_803_9_11_committee_act.pdf; https://it.ojp.gov/default.aspx?page=1283.
45 (U) The Commission on the Intelligence Capabilities of the United States Regarding Weapons of Mass Destruction (WMD Commission), *Report to the President,* March 31, 2005, http://fas.org/irp/offdocs/wmd_report.pdf (accessed on December 11, 2014): 331.

26

operations."[46] Instead, the WMD Commission asserted that "all three national security missions—intelligence, counterintelligence, and counterterrorism—should be jointly managed at the strategic level and fully integrated in planning, targeting, and operations."[47]

(U) The WMD Commission recommended to the President "an organizational reform of the FBI that pulls all of its intelligence capabilities into one place and subjects them to the coordinating authority of the DNI."[48] By recommending the consolidation of the FBI's Counterterrorism and Counterintelligence Divisions (CTD and CD) and the DI within a single National Security Service under a single senior FBI official, the WMD Commission linked intelligence and investigations in counterterrorism and counterintelligence but was effectively recommending the demotion of the head of intelligence within the FBI. This forced the EAD responsible for counterterrorism and counterintelligence investigations to also be responsible for intelligence activities for those two areas. But this arguably made more difficult the FBI's efforts to improve the status of intelligence analysts, even as the WMD Commission identified improving analytic capability as one of the three areas where the FBI had made insufficient progress in its intelligence work.[49] To this day, the FBI has not promoted or hired an intelligence analyst to a level above deputy assistant director. Nevertheless, while the DI was structurally assigned within the National Security Branch (NSB), the directorate continued to have responsibility for the management of the intelligence program across all parts of the Bureau.[50]

(U) The President directed the creation of a National Security Service under a senior FBI official on June 28, 2005.[51] The FBI shortly thereafter stood up the NSB under a single EAD, a special agent executive whose sole FBI experience was in criminal investigation.[52] The FBI continued to evolve as other parts of the Federal Government were also going through significant changes. Among other recommendations of the 9/11 Commission codified by the Congress in IRPTA that related to the transformation of the FBI, the establishment of the National Counterterrorism Center (NCTC) was perhaps the most important with respect to counterterrorism.[53] The 9/11 Commission recommended that this center be based on the existing Terrorist Threat Integration Center (TTIC) and combine strategic intelligence and joint operational planning, staffed by personnel from various agencies.[54] As established by Congress, the Senate-confirmed NCTC director was to serve as the principal adviser to the Director of National Intelligence on intelligence operations relating to counterterrorism and provide strategic operational plans, including "effective integration of counterterrorism intelligence and operations across agency

---

46 (U) WMD Commission, *Letters to the President on FBI and CIA Transformation Plans*, March 29, 2005, http://govinfo.library.unt.edu/wmb/report/fbicia/pdf (accessed on January 9, 2015).
47 (U) Ibid.
48 (U) Ibid., 3.
49 (U) Ibid., 454. The other two areas were validation of human sources of intelligence and information technology.
50 (U) See *FBI Intelligence Strategy, 2014-2018*.
51 (U) CNN. "Bush Creates National Security Service," http://www.cnn.com2005/POLITICS/06/29/bush.intel (accessed on December 11, 2014).
52 (U) See Electronic Communication, September 12, 2005. The senior intelligence officer who had served as EAD for Intelligence left the Bureau. The NSB EADs were not intelligence professionals. See http://www.justice.gov/oig/special0506/chapter6.htm.
53 (U) See Section 1021 of IRTPA.
54 (U) *The 9/11 Commission Report*, 403.

boundaries, both inside and outside the United States."[55] FBI personnel from CTD were assigned to the NCTC. Additional collaboration was facilitated when the CTD, NCTC, and the CIA's CTC moved resources into the same state-of-the-art office building in Northern Virginia.

(U) As these changes were being implemented, at the request of Congressman Frank Wolf, chairman of the Commerce, Justice, Science and Related Agencies Subcommittee on the House Appropriations subcommittee (CJSR), the National Academy of Public Administration (NAPA) conducted reviews of the FBI's operations.[56] The NAPA panel had endorsed the thrust of Director Mueller's priorities and reorganization efforts in 2002 and 2003. In 2005, the NAPA panel reported that it, "like the 9/11 Commission, is convinced that the FBI is making substantial progress in transforming itself into a strong domestic intelligence entity, and has the will and many of the competencies required to accomplish it."[57] Nevertheless, the panel had 37 recommendations for the FBI related to transformation, counterterrorism, intelligence, and security.

(U) In late 2005, the 9/11 Public Discourse Project, formed by the 10 members of the 9/11 Commission, issued reports on the progress made by the government in implementing the 9/11 Commission's recommendations. Amid grades ranging from "B" to "F", the 9/11 Public Discourse ranked the creation of the FBI national security workforce as "C". It found progress was being made "but it is too slow." In addition, the 9/11 Public Discourse Project expressed concern that there were still "significant deficiencies in the FBI's analytic capability" and that "initiatives to improve information technology capabilities have failed."[58]

(U) Further work reviewing the FBI's transformation was done by the Congressional Research Service. It had begun a series of reviews after 9/11, some also at the request of Chairman Wolf.[59] Its attention to the FBI's counterterrorism mission continues today.[60] DOJ's Office of the Inspector General also conducted oversight of FBI's national security activities.[61] The FBI's

---

55 (U) Section 119 of the National Security Act of 1947 (50 U.S.C. § 404 *et. seq.*).

56 (U) See, A Report of a Panel of the National Academy of Public Administration for the U.S. Congress and the Federal Bureau of Investigation, *Transforming the FBI: Progress and Challenges,* January 2005. The NAPA panel was chartered to review the FBI's "divisional reorganizations and major process, personnel, and cultural changes." It endorsed the thrust of Director Mueller's priorities and reorganization in 2002 with recommendations to "improve the prospects of success."

57 (U) Ibid., xi.

58 (U) 9/11 Public Discourse Project, *Report on the Status of 9/11 Commission Recommendations, Part II: Reforming the Institutions of Government,* December 5, 2005, http://www.npr.org/documents/2005/dec/9-11_commission/2005-12-05_report.pdf (accessed on December 11, 2014): 2.

59 (U) See, e.g., Alfred Cummings and Todd Masse, *Intelligence Reform Implementation at Federal Bureau of Investigation; Issues and Options for Congress*, (Congressional Research Service, August 16, 2005) RL33033.

60 (U) See, e.g., Jerome P. Bjelopera, *The Federal Bureau of Investigation and Terrorism Investigations*, (Congressional Research Service, February 19, 2014).

61 (U) See http://www.justice.gov/oig/reports/fbi.htm, including: Department of Justice Office of Inspector General, *A Review of the Federal Bureau of Investigation's Use of Exigent Letters and Other Informal Requests for Telephone Records*, January 2010 (November 24, 2013 version); Department of Justice Office of Inspector General, *A Review of the Handling and Storage of Information Prior to the April 15, 2013 Boston Bombings* (Unclassified Summary); April 10, 2014, and Department of Justice Office of Inspector General, *Audit of the Federal Bureau of Investigation Management of Terrorist Watchlist Nominations (Redacted version)*, Audit Report 14-16 (March 25, 2014). In addition, the Government Accountability Office (GAO) conducted audits and reviews of FBI activities,

production of intelligence reports dramatically increased, although questions continued to be raised about quality control.[62]

(U) Further Refinement and Lessons Learned

(U) Even after implementing these changes in 2001–2005, the FBI continued to seek ways to achieve its goals more effectively. The CTD in 2005 sought lessons from business management theories to improve its practices. CTD developed what it called a strategy map by which it could "communicate its strategy, prioritize initiatives, measure progress, and identify each person's role in pursuing the Division's strategy."[63] The strategy map identified the intelligence cycle as the core of the FBI's internal process.[64] In 2006, Director Mueller asked the EAD for criminal investigations, who had participated in the CTD process, and a team of other senior executives to build a strategy map for the FBI as a whole.

(U) By 2007, the team created such a map with 25 objectives in four categories. Director Mueller then established a Strategic Execution Team (SET) "to build the FBI's intelligence capabilities and make intelligence more central in FBI operations."[65] The effort involved more than 100 special agents, intelligence analysts, and other personnel from Headquarters and dozens of field offices. The SET started with intelligence operations in the field offices and development of human capital for intelligence. It also took on management of transformation efforts and initiatives within the FBI.[66]

(U) The SET process sought to standardize and upgrade the FIGs, with best practices identified for small, medium, and large offices; and produced a training program for agents, supervisors, and executives in the 56 field offices by the end of 2008. The SET also sought to ensure non-special agent personnel were "as capable of and devoted to completing the intelligence cycle as FBI agents had traditionally been capable of and devoted to closing criminal cases."[67] The FBI increased its recruiting and training efforts and made clearer how intelligence analysts would progress through their careers. The FBI also identified 12 key focus areas including leadership and resource management to achieve the goal of being "a threat-based, intelligence-driven

---

see, e.g., Government Accountability Office, *FBI Counterterrorism: Vacancies Have Declined, but FBI Has Not Assessed the Long-Term Sustainability of Its Strategy for Addressing Vacancies* (April, 2012).

62 (U) The FBI's production of IIRs saw a fourfold increase between FY2006 and FY2014. ; Memorandum for the Record, August 11, 2014.; Memorandum for the Record, November 11, 2014.

63 (U) Jan W. Rivkin, Michael Roberto, Ranjay Gulati, *Harvard Business School Case Study: Federal Bureau of Investigation, 2009,* 9-710-452 (*HBS Case Study*) (Revised May 18, 2010): 1.

64 (U) The four key elements of the intelligence cycle are requirements, collection, analysis, dissemination.

65 (U) *HBS Case Study*, 3.

66 (U) *HBS Case Study*, 4. The head of the effort stated, "For a while after 9/11, it seemed that someone in the FBI would launch a new change effort every month. In the field, the workforce was exhausted and, because agents and analysts couldn't tell the difference between efforts that would be sustained and those that wouldn't, they became skeptical of all the efforts. With each initiative, they assumed that 'This too shall pass.' SET aimed to focus on fewer initiatives but to push each one harder."

67 (U) *HBS Case Study*, 4.

organization" and now describes itself this way in congressional testimony and internal briefings.[68]

(U) The FBI, working with other federal entities, continued to establish new entities and reorganize to address terrorism and cross-border issues. In July 2006 it established a Weapons of Mass Destruction Directorate (WMDD) within the NSB to integrate all FBI components working on WMD issues. The Terrorist Screening Center (TSC), which had been established in 2003, was brought under the NSB in 2008. The FBI was made the executive agent for the new High-Value Detainee Interrogation Group (HIG) in 2010, established with the Department of Defense (DOD) and the CIA to ensure that interrogation expertise and resources from across the government would be available for deployment on an immediate basis for the interrogation of certain high-value detainees.

(U) The period from late 2008 to 2010 was a period of intense challenge for counterterrorism within the FBI and the USIC. Among the significant terrorism events that brought the FBI's counterterrorism capabilities into play were: the Mumbai attack of November 2008 and the eventual arrest of David Coleman Headley; the tracking and arrest of Najibullah Zazi and his associates in late summer 2009; the attack on US military personnel at Fort Hood by Major Nidal Hassan in November 2009; and the attempted Times Square bombing by Faisal Shahzad on May 1, 2010. (These cases and the Boston Marathon Bombing of April 2013 are discussed in Chapter II.)[69] At the same time, however, FBI offices were also conducting much lower-profile operations to detect and disrupt terrorist attacks within the United States.[70] The FBI was also simultaneously conducting criminal investigations from simple bank robberies to complex white collar criminal conspiracies.[71]

(U) The Fort Hood attack in 2009 prompted intense scrutiny of the USG's failure to act in ways that might have prevented Army Major Nidal Hasan from the mass shooting that left 13 DOD employees dead and another 32 wounded in the worst terrorist attack within the United States since September 11, 2001. The chairman and ranking member of the US Senate Homeland Security and Governmental Affairs Committee issued their special report, *A Ticking Time Bomb: Counterterrorism Lessons from the U.S. Government's Failure to Prevent the Fort Hood Attack,* on February 3, 2011. While acknowledging that the detection and interdiction of terrorists who

---

68 (U) *The Evolution of the National Security Branch*, 2. The other metrics include measurement of success; information sharing; intelligence community; scope; internal and external communications; organization; human capital; workforce culture; and information technology. See *FBI Intelligence Program* (2014); James B. Comey, Statement before the House Appropriations Committee, Subcommittee on Commerce, Justice, Science, and Related Agencies, Washington, D.C., March 26, 2014. (*Comey testimony*).

69 (U) In addition to these four high-profile cases and the April 2013 Boston bombing discussed in a later section of this report, the FBI also responded to Umar Farouk Abdulmutallab's attempt to bring down a US airliner on December 25, 2009; AQAP operative Ahmed Abdulkadir Warsame and a number of other investigations, such as those into Somali pirates; and Mansour J. Arbabsiar, the Iranian-American charged with plotting to kill the Saudi Ambassador.

70 (U) *The Threat Matrix*, 3-10, 596-597 (four sting operations in which young men planned to detonate explosives at different locations around the country); (monitoring the 2009 Presidential Inauguration threat stream).

71 (U) *The Threat Matrix*, 598 (noting the following "huge cases" during Director Mueller's tenure of "Enron, Global Crossing, Bernard Madoff, Russian spy rings, drug and gang-related cases of mind-goggling complexity," as well as more than "60,000 bank robberies, and 2,000 civil rights cases," among others.)

act alone is one of the most difficult challenges facing law enforcement and intelligence agencies, the Committee found that the DOD and FBI "collectively had sufficient information to have detected Hasan's radicalization to violent Islamist extremism but failed to understand and to act on it."[72] The report found that "The FBI has made significant strides since 9/11 in transforming itself into America's lead counterterrorism agency and an intelligence-driven organization to prevent terrorist attacks domestically, but it is clear from the Hasan case that the transformation is incomplete."[73]

(U) Senators Lieberman and Collins, in their committee report, found that the FBI's handling of information that it had concerning Hasan was "impeded by division among its field offices, insufficient use of intelligence analysis, and outdated tradecraft."[74] In addition, they found that the inquiry into Hasan was "focused on the narrow question of whether he was engaged in terrorist activities and not whether he was radicalizing to violent Islamist extremism and could thus become a threat."[75] Looking at the interaction between the FBI and the DOD, they were also concerned that the FBI's JTTFs were not fully effective "interagency coordination and information-sharing mechanisms" and that the question of lead responsibility for counterterrorism investigations of service members was unresolved between the FBI and DOD.[76] Senators Lieberman and Collins made detailed recommendations for the FBI and the DOD, some of which were instituted at the FBI during the Congressional investigation.[77]

(U) FBI Director Mueller also commissioned former FBI Director Webster to review issues involving the FBI's counterterrorism program, including whether its authorities were sufficient. Judge Webster and his commission presented their final report to the Director in late 2011, including their assessment of FBI's ongoing remedial actions, an analysis of FBI's governing authorities, and recommendations for additional steps the FBI should take with a particular focus on the FBI's information technology.[78]

(U) On October 1, 2008, a full year before the Fort Hood attack on November 19, 2009, Attorney General Michael Mukasey issued new guidelines for domestic FBI operations (AG Guidelines). These new AG Guidelines replaced five sets of guidelines that had separately addressed, among other matters, criminal investigations, national security investigations, and foreign intelligence collection.[79] Significantly, the new AG Guidelines represented a single set of guidelines that applied to FBI activities within the United States, regardless of whether the

---

72 (U) Joseph I. Lieberman, Chairman, and Susan M. Collins, Ranking Member, the Senate Homeland Security and Government Affairs Committee, *A Ticking Time Bomb: Counterterrorism Lessons from the U.S. Government's Failure to Prevent the Fort Hood Attack (A Ticking Time Bomb)* (February, 2011), 7.
73 (U) *A Ticking Time Bomb,* 51.
74 (U) Ibid., 55.
75 (U) Ibid., 66.
76 (U) Ibid., 67.
77 (U) See Electronic Communication, August 2, 2011.
78 (U) *Final Report of the William H. Webster Commission on The Federal Bureau of Investigation, Counterterrorism Intelligence, and the Events at Fort Hood, Texas, on November 5, 2009 (Webster Commission Report)* (Undated).
79 (U) Valerie Caproni, General Counsel, Federal Bureau of Investigation, *Statement before the Senate Select Committee on Intelligence, (Caproni Testimony),* September 23, 2008.

purpose was counterterrorism, counterintelligence, or criminal investigation.[80] The FBI explicitly saw these consolidated guidelines as reflecting "the FBI's status as a full-fledged intelligence collection agency and member of the United States Intelligence Community"[81] as well as helping the FBI in its "transformation from the preeminent law enforcement agency in the United States to a domestic intelligence agency that has a national security mission and law enforcement mission."[82]

(U) The FBI had requested the Attorney General to consider revisions to the guidelines in 2007, in part because the FBI "believed that certain restrictions [in the prior National Security Investigative Guidelines, last revised in 2003] were actively interfering with its ability to . . . become an intelligence-driven agency capable of anticipating and preventing terrorist and other criminal acts as well as investigating them after they are committed."[83] While the new AG Guidelines continued the distinction between predicated investigations and pre-investigative activity, known as "threat assessments" on the national security side and "prompt and limited checking of leads" on the criminal side, substantively the new AG Guidelines represented an expansion in the range of techniques available at the pre-investigative level for national security and intelligence matters, bringing consistency to the rules "whether the activity has as its purpose checking on potential criminal activity, examining a potential threat to national security, or collecting foreign intelligence in response to a requirement."[84]

(U) With the new and almost entirely unclassified AG Guidelines, special agents working on national security issues could now at the assessment stage "recruit and task sources, engage in interviews of members of the public without a requirement to identify themselves as FBI agents and disclose the precise purpose of the interview, and engage in physical surveillance not requiring a court order"[85] just as special agents working on organized crime investigations could do.[86]

(U) The new AG Guidelines carried over substantial privacy and civil liberties protections from earlier investigative guidelines and also contained new requirements for notifications and reports by the FBI to improve oversight of the Bureau's national security and intelligence activities.[87] The five case studies in Chapter II of this report assess the FBI's effectiveness in applying these guidelines and in its use of intelligence collection and analysis in the investigations of each case.

---

80 (U) The underlying guidelines for these three areas had already been revised successfully in 2002, 2003, and 2006. *Caproni Testimony,* 2.

81 (U) Ibid., 3.

82 (U) Ibid., 1. The Webster Commission found that "the increased flexibility under the AG Guidelines to conduct assessments using specified techniques is critical to the FBI's ability to combat terrorism." *Webster Commission Report,* 109.

83 (U) *Caproni Testimony,* 3.

84 (U) Ibid., 2.

85 (U) Ibid.

86 (U) Ibid., 6-7.

87 (U) Ibid., 7-9. The AG Guidelines were implemented within the Bureau according to the FBI's Domestic Investigations and Operations Guide (DIOG) which was issued by the FBI Director in 2008, with some modifications made in 2010 and 2013. The FBI requires all of its operation personnel to complete comprehensive training on the AG Guidelines and the DIOG.

(U) Leadership Transition and 10 Years after the 9/11 Commission Recommendations

(U) The FBI continued to make efforts to advance its intelligence activities during the last years of Mueller's tenure.[88] Some of this effort involved sustained discussion of its intelligence mission although reports regarding its accomplishments were limited to traditional measures of a law enforcement organization such as 25,186 arrests; 14,807 indictments; 1,147 missing children located; and $1,125 billion in seizures of drugs and assets. While the 2013-2014 Today's FBI report did not provide exact information regarding the FBI's intelligence program, it did devote six pages to explaining the Bureau's intelligence and national security activities before describing its investigations, people, partnerships, and services.[89]

(U) Pursuant to the FY10 Intelligence Authorization Act, P.L. 111-259, the FBI was required to provide annual classified reports to Congress for five years concerning its ongoing transformation of intelligence capabilities within the FBI. In its third report, submitted in April 2013, the NSB described the completion of a "comprehensive review of the FBI's intelligence program and the implementation of recommendations to streamline the organization while positioning it to more effectively collect, analyze, produce, and disseminate intelligence."[90]

(U) This intelligence program review led to a reorganization of the DI and the transfer of functions—including domain management, collection management, targeting, tactical analysis, strategic analysis, and finished intelligence production—from the DI to intelligence personnel who have been embedded within the FBI Headquarters (FBIHQ) operational divisions.[91] The 2013 assessment report noted that threat-based fusion cells within the operational divisions "serve as intelligence teams to integrate all aspects of the intelligence cycle, providing a more strategic and nimble approach to identifying and mitigating current and emerging threats."[92] To implement this approach, the FBI did a comprehensive revision of its Intelligence Program Policy Guide and established a DI Executive Advisory Group. In 2014, Director Comey elevated the position of the incumbent Director of Intelligence to Executive Assistant Director for Intelligence.

(U) In addition, according to the 2013 report, between 2012 and 2013, the FBI developed and implemented the Integrated Program Management (IPM) to standardize processes between FBIHQ and the field on how to prioritize threats, allocate resources, and measure performance. Coupled with this, the FBI at both the Headquarters and field level continued to utilize the Threat Review and Prioritization (TRP) process for prioritizing threats and mitigation strategies on both

---

88 (U) The former director's tenure was extended two years by an act of Congress.
89 (U) Federal Bureau of Investigation, *Today's FBI: Facts & Figures 2013-2014 (Today's FBI)* http://www.fbi.gov/stats-services/publications/todays-fbi-facts-figures/facts-and-figures-031413.pdf (accessed on January 12, 2015).
90 (U) Federal Bureau of Investigation, *Assessment of the Progress on the Transformation of the Intelligence Capabilities of the Federal Bureau of Investigation (Assessment Report)* (April, 2013): 1.
91 (U) Ibid., 3.
92 (U) Ibid.

the national and local level, to ensure FBIHQ had a national threat picture, as the threats were emerging and distributed across the country.[93]

(U) In the 2013 report, the FBI noted it had increased its production of raw intelligence reports over the last year. The report stated that, during FY12, "48 percent of FBI's finished intelligence products received "Good" or "Excellent" ratings on each of the four analytic Integrity Standards criteria, and 95 percent of intelligence products were disseminated in a timely manner."[94] The FBI conducted an Intelligence Analyst Workforce Study (IAWS), after which decided to retain the organization's nonsupervisory GS-14 Intelligence Analyst position and implement a new IA developmental plan.[95] The report also addressed issues involving infrastructure support and the technical backbone of the Intelligence Program and the integration of the NSB into the USIC.[96]

(U) The FBI's budget authority increased from $3.81 billion in FY01 to $8.12 billion in FY12.[97] Despite the growth of budget authority since FY01, in recent years the FBI faced complex threats with reduced funds, in part as a result of sequestration. In a May 2014 speech, FBI Deputy Director Mark F. Giuliano noted that the Bureau had been cutting programs during the last few fiscal years, and so its allocation of $8.3 billion in FY14 was a "relief."[98]

(U) The April 2013 report concluded:

> Today, the FBI is an intelligence-driven organization that is more efficiently and effectively using intelligence to drive operations. Significant advancements have been made in many areas over the past year to ensure the FBI is positioned to meet its missions with the constraints of budgetary reductions. The work continues to become more streamlined and standardized across the enterprise through leveraging new technology, working in tandem with partner agencies on common missions, and the ongoing development of FBI personnel.[99]

(U) The Review Commission has examined several of these initiatives to test how effective they have been. Our findings and recommendations highlight where resources can be targeted more efficiently and effectively and where new strategic plans must be implemented strategically and smoothly to move the FBI forward.[100]

---

93 (U) It was recognized, however, that there could be variations among field offices in how their priorities were ranked as the TRP process reflects the intelligence or "domain management" responsibilities of the individual field offices. It also represents a mechanism to be "threat-driven."

94 (U) *Assessment Report*, 8. The methods by which the FBI measures timeliness should be reviewed. See discussion in footnote 272. The Assessment Report includes discussion of efforts made to increase the quality of FBI reporting.

95 (U) Ibid., 10-16.

96 (U) Ibid., 16-21.

97 (U) *Today's FBI*, 9.

98 (U) Mark F. Giuliano, *Statement for the Record* (Washington Institute for Near East Policy, May 28, 2014): 1.

99 (U) *Assessment Report*, 22.

100 (U) While the FBI's budget allocation grew this year, additional budget growth is not a given. If recommendations are made to increase resources in some areas, recommendations might also be made to eliminate certain activities.

(U) Baseline 2015

(U) On March 26, 2014, new FBI Director James Comey, in testimony on the FBI's budget request for FY15 before the CJSR, stated that "[t]oday's FBI is a threat-focused, intelligence-driven organization." According to Director Comey's testimony, the FBI's four priorities "remain focused on defending the United States against terrorism, foreign intelligence, and cyber threats; upholding and enforcing the criminal laws of the United States; protecting civil rights and civil liberties; and providing leadership and criminal justice services to federal, state, municipal, and international agencies and partners."[101]

(U) The Review Commission concludes that the FBI has transformed itself over the last 10 years, in alignment with the Director's four priorities. The Bureau is developing a cadre of special agents, analysts, and other professionals who understand the importance of intelligence across the spectrum of FBI operations. Nevertheless, we believe the FBI has not yet met its potential—or its mandate from the President and Congress—to develop a "specialized and integrated national security workforce" that can serve as the hub of America's domestic intelligence agency.[102] Furthermore, we believe that the increasing gravity of transnational security threats in an era of rapid technological change requires stronger efforts by the FBI to optimize its capabilities and to maximize its collaboration with strategic partners. The following current challenges noted by the Review Commission rest on the durable foundation—the baseline—of the Mueller years but argue for even more accelerated reform in the decade ahead.

(U) Intelligence: The Review Commission concludes that that the FBI's capability to collect and analyze intelligence in support of its investigative mission has improved over the past decade but support for national intelligence level requirements is still a work in progress. FBI analysts and special agents continue to perform admirably as detailees to United States Intelligence Community USIC agencies and at foreign posts. The majority of strategic analysis and engagement with the USIC is conducted at headquarters through the threat-based fusion cells within the operational divisions. But analysts and collectors in FBI field offices, with some exceptions, do not collaborate closely enough with USIC counterparts or produce strategic analysis related to their area of responsibility that is informed by USIC intelligence traffic and production. This results, in part, from the lack of adequate Sensitive Compartmental Information Facilities (SCIF) space needed for FBI employees to have desk-top access to USIC systems, tools, and message traffic—and the analysts who produce it. The inability to fully integrate into the USIC reduces their professional status both within the Bureau and the USIC, as well as their effectiveness in producing strategic—versus tactical—analysis in response to field office and USIC requirements. Well conceived programs intended to boost intelligence capacity, such as

---

101 (U) *Comey Testimony.*

102 (U) *The 9/11 Commission Report,* 425. In our interviews and briefings, no one has told us the FBI has achieved 100 percent in doing all that is necessary to be an intelligence institution. Indeed, Director Comey on June 4, 2014, identified intelligence as one of his three top priorities as the new director because the integration of intelligence and operations "is going okay, but it is not going nearly well enough." Message from Director Comey to FBI workforce, June 4, 2014. He thus created a new Intelligence Branch to drive the integration of intelligence and operations across the bureau and institute coordinated training for special agents and new intelligence analysts to promote better integration in the field.

HUMINT squads and Central Strategic Coordinating Components (CSCC), struggle in the field in part because of local leadership's choices amid competing priorities.

(U) Leadership: Leadership at all levels of the FBI impacts this pace of change by advancing it or slowing it down. The workforce grasps the FBI's stated intention to transform itself into an intelligence-driven, threat-based organization, but implementation across the Bureau varies widely. The Review Commission observed a variety of leaders at Headquarters and in the field, who were all committed to the Bureau's mission as they understand it. Still, interviews and comments from leaders in the field reflected a wide range of responses from high-energy change agents to passive resistors with regard to the goal of an integrated intelligence and law-enforcement mission. In the Bureau's critical years ahead, visionary leadership will matter more than ever.

(U) Analysis as a Profession: The Bureau, despite its stated intentions to address concerns from its analysts over time, still does not sufficiently recognize its analysts as a professionalized workforce with distinct requirements for investment in training and education, rotational opportunities across the USIC, and a career service that will meet both the professional expectations of analysts and the growing needs of a global service.

(U) Information Sharing: The FBI's information sharing practices and collaborative relationships are markedly improved from a decade ago. But there is still wide room for improvement in the Bureau's sharing practices with local law enforcement and the private sector. Looking ahead, the FBI will be increasingly dependent upon all domestic and foreign partnerships to succeed in its critical and growing national security missions—including against the rapidly evolving cyber and terrorist threats.

(U) LEGAT Program: The challenges to the Bureau's core missions—criminal investigation, intelligence, and technology—are already and will be increasingly global. The Bureau's LEGAT program is growing—today's 64 LEGAT offices represent a three-fold increase since the early 1990s—and will be required to grow strategically and smartly over the next decade. Investing in the LEGAT program for both criminal investigation and intelligence collection is wise, but there are growing pains as the various offices exhibit. The Bureau requires clearer goals for designating priority countries to assign LEGATs, for candidate selection, for enhanced training and education, for standardization of business processes, and especially expanding analytic capability, including analysts embedded in the LEGAT offices. The recently announced plan for the LEGAT program's reorganization, which includes enhanced analytic capability, is an encouraging step as long as it receives commensurate resources.

(U) Science and Technology (S&T): The FBI has substantially increased its investment in its S&T programs over the past decade. The Review Commission heard insightful briefings from the FBI's Science and Technology Branch (Operational Technology Division, Laboratory Division, and Criminal Justice Information Services Division) on its ambitious efforts to keep apace of rapid advances in IT, biometrics, DNA applications, forensics, and other sciences that relate to both the special agent's investigative tradecraft and the adversary's capabilities. S&T should be seen as a core competency of the Bureau in future planning and resource allocation in the midst of a global technological revolution of unprecedented scale and scope. The FBI will need to strengthen its outreach to the scientific community and increase the S&T Branch's "touch points" with internal divisions, field offices, and LEGAT posts.

(U) Strategic Plan: The FBI today does not have a comprehensive strategic vision or overall plan to integrate the national and international responsibilities for a global threat-based, intelligence-driven investigative organization. Some of the problems that complicate the effort to develop such a long-term plan are problems that the Bureau can fix on its own, including the uneven commitment of its leadership to reform. However, it also is hindered by the Bureau's one-year budget cycle, which contrasts with the Defense budget five-year cycle by which the majority of USIC members are funded. The FBI's bifurcated budget process runs through the contrasting evaluations of DOJ and ODNI budget offices and then on to Congressional committees of jurisdiction, also similarly divided between intelligence and law enforcement interests. This is a discouraging and frustrating picture for a Bureau mandated to integrate what its overseers view through separate lenses.

(U) Legal Authorities and Civil Liberties: The FBI faces constitutional and legal challenges in collecting intelligence and rendering analysis of US persons' information that distinguish it from other USIC agencies. The Review Commission's assessment of five recent, high-profile counterterrorism cases highlights the critical value of the FBI's existing authorities and related statutes and performance in detecting and countering the terrorist threat. The Electronic Communications Privacy Act (ECPA), Communications Assistance for Law Enforcement Act (CALEA), the Foreign Intelligence Surveillance Act (FISA), and the USA PATRIOT Act were all essential to the investigations in each case. The FBI should ensure Congress is aware of the critical value of these programs as it considers retaining, refining, and expanding the Bureau's authorities as the threat evolves. The Bureau also must ensure that, in an escalating threat environment, its internal safeguards to protect civil liberties meet the highest standard.

CHAPTER II
THE SUM OF FIVE CASES

(U) The 9/11 Review Commission selected five case studies to examine the Bureau's response to high-profile terrorist plots and attacks since 2008. These cases are briefly summarized in the box below: Najibullah Zazi and the New York City subway plot, David Headley and the Mumbai attack and Denmark plot, Major Nidal Hasan and the Fort Hood shooting, Faisal Shahzad and the Times Square attack, and Tamerlan and Dzhokhar Tsarnaev and the Boston Marathon bombing. The Review Commission concludes that FBI's human intelligence (HUMINT), intelligence analysis, and information sharing practices performed unevenly in the five cases to varying degrees. In addition, the Review Commission believes, looking forward, counterterrorism legal authorities under the Foreign Intelligence Surveillance Act (FISA) and other statutory authorities afforded to the FBI are essential to its ability to fulfill its national security mission.

(U) Key Points

- (U) In none of the five cases did an FBI confidential human source (CHS) provide actionable intelligence to help prevent or respond to a terrorist operation. In no case, despite the existence of a functioning HUMINT program, did FBI human sources alert the FBI to the plotters.

- (U) Intelligence analysts embedded in counterterrorism squads were valued for the tactical intelligence support they provided for the cases, but domain intelligence needs to be enhanced to identify plots in the relevant field offices' area of responsibility and intelligence analysts must be empowered to question special agents' operational assumptions.

- (U) The case studies identify lapses in communication, coordination, and collaboration among Joint Terrorism Task Forces (JTTFs) in FBI field offices; between FBI Headquarters and the field; and between the Bureau and its federal, state, and local partners in law enforcement and intelligence.

- (U) FBI authorities derived from the Electronic Communications Privacy Act (ECPA), the FISA, and the USA PATRIOT Act, as well as Communications Assistance for Law Enforcement Act (CALEA)'s mandate for specific communications companies, were pivotal in the investigation of all five cases.

(U) Snapshot of the Five Cases

(U) Najibullah Zazi

In September 2009, outside of Denver, Colorado, the FBI arrested then 24-year old Najibullah Zazi, a Pakistan-born US citizen, for his role in a core al-Qa'ida plot to conduct suicide attacks on the New York City subway. Along with two associates, Zarein Ahmedzay and Adis Medunjanin, Zazi met with al-Qa'ida leaders in Pakistan in 2008 to plan the attacks and conduct training.

(U) David Headley

David Headley, a then 49-year old US citizen of Pakistani heritage, was arrested by the FBI in October 2009 for his planning and involvement in a core al-Qa'ida plot to attack the Morgenavisen Jyllands-Posten newspaper in Copenhagen, Denmark. Headley had also played a major role in providing intelligence, surveillance, and reconnaissance support to the 2008 Lashkar-e-Taiba terrorist attack in Mumbai, India. With the help of his friend Tahawwur Rana and Rana's business operations based in Chicago, Headley was able to conduct his activities overseas.

(U) Nidal Hasan

Nidal Hasan, 39, a US citizen and a major in the US Army, shot to death 13 people and wounded 32 others on November 19, 2009, at the Soldier Readiness Center in Fort Hood, Texas. Hasan, who was told he would be deployed to Afghanistan, had been in regular e-mail contact with al-Qa'ida in the Arabian Peninsula operative Anwar al-Aulaqi, who was based in Yemen.

(U) Faisal Shahzad

On May 1, 2010, Faisal Shahzad, 30, a Pakistani-born US citizen, drove his Nissan Pathfinder into Times Square in New York City and attempted to detonate an improvised explosive device. Shahzad had received training and other support from Tehreek-e-Taliban leaders in Pakistan. The bomb failed to explode. After a round the clock manhunt, Shahzad was arrested on May 3, 2010, as he attempted to flee the United States.

(U) Tamerlan and Dzhokhar Tsarnaev

On April 15, 2013, Kyrgyzstan-born US citizen Dzhokhar Tsarnaev and Russia-born LPR Tamerlan Tsarnaev, 27 and 19, bombed the Boston Marathon, killing three people and injuring nearly 300 others. They had radicalized, in part, by listening to on-line sermons of jihadists, including al-Qa'ida operative Anwar al-Aulaqi. The Tsarnaevs utilized such publications as *Inspire* magazine to help construct the bombs.

(U) The Review Commission chose these cases—and the case study approach more broadly—for two principal reasons. First, they helped us to measure the FBI's counterterrorism performance against its professed goal to be a threat-based, intelligence-driven organization. The FBI's counterterrorism mission has been a major beneficiary of increased intelligence support over the past decade. Accordingly, by reviewing these five cases, we were able to assess the impact that both these policy changes and additional resources have had on the FBI's counterterrorism mission. Second, the case studies enabled us to identify specific issues that need to be addressed by the FBI to fulfill its role as the central hub of US domestic intelligence—integrating federal, state, local, and tribal law enforcement and intelligence capabilities, as well as liaison with the private sector, local communities, and foreign partners.

The Review Commission discovered that building this collaborative enterprise is still a work in progress for the FBI, with inconsistency from case to case.

(U) Each of the five cases presented different complexities, allowing the Review Commission to consider various factors that affected the FBI's performance. Hasan and the Tsarnaevs were able to carry out their terrorist attacks. Zazi was arrested in Denver before he and his accomplices could execute their suicide attack on the New York City subway. Headley was detained in Chicago after he had already played a pivotal role in the Mumbai attacks, but before he could return to Denmark to support another terrorist operation. Shahzad's plan to detonate an improvised explosive device in New York City's crowded Times Square was undermined merely because of his own incompetence. The perpetrators were all either US citizens or permanent residents, and diverged sharply in their respective family and personal relationships, social networks, and radicalization experiences. Moreover, in each instance the role of the FBI, local law enforcement organizations, and national and foreign intelligence agencies in identifying and investigating the perpetrators also differed. The cases also include significant variation in the nature and intent of extremist groups and networks, with plotters connected to terrorist organizations (such as core al-Qa'ida, Tehrik-e-Taliban Pakistan (TTP), and Lashkar-e-Taiba (LeT)) and local radicalized individuals and networks.

(U) For each of the case studies, the Review Commission conducted site visits and interviews with many of the FBI field office and Headquarters personnel responsible for the intelligence and investigative processes, reviewed hundreds of documents, and interviewed dozens of individuals involved in the cases from United States Intelligence Community (USIC) partner agencies.[103] The Review Commission did not duplicate the investigative and intelligence work completed by the Justice Department, the FBI, or USIC partners. Nor did the Review Commission re-create the after-action reports produced by the FBI, Inspectors General, USIC, or Congress.

(U) Instead, we focused on the strengths and weaknesses in four areas integral to successful FBI counterterrorism operations: (1) HUMINT collection; (2) intelligence analysis; (3) communication, collaboration, and information sharing involving the JTTFs; and (4) counterterrorism legal authorities. These areas provided an overarching framework to guide our interviews and the collection of information for each of the five cases. We examined the FBI's performance in each to identify both the challenges and opportunities to improve performance against evolving threats. Although these five cases were the principal focus of this effort, the Review Commission was nonetheless mindful that other terrorist incidents were prevented by the FBI since 2001, such as those involving Michael Finton, Hosam Maher Husein Smadi, the DC 5, Daniel Boyd and his accomplices, Tarek Mehanna, Farooq Chaudry, Colleen LaRose, Zachary Chesser, and numerous others.[104]

---

103 (U) Importantly, the Review Commission was not able to discuss the Boston Marathon bombing during our visit to Boston due to ongoing preparations for the Tsarnaev trial, although we did address issues pertaining to HUMINT, intelligence analysis, JTTFs, and counterterrorism authorities more broadly during our visit. The Boston case was the only one where the Review Commission relied primarily on Inspectors' General reports, outside interviews, and open source reporting, due to FBI restrictions on discussing the case while the trial is pending.
104 (U) For a more detailed list on interdicted terrorism plots see Bruce Hoffman and Peter Bergen, *Assessing the Terrorist Threat,* Bipartisan Policy Center, September 10, 2010: 33-37.

(U) The Review Commission cannot say that with better JTTF collaboration, HUMINT, or even intelligence analysis that the FBI would have detected these plots beforehand. Rather, the Review Commission used the case studies as a lens through which to review the FBI's progress in these areas. The plots, all of which crossed multiple field offices or included overseas components, might have benefitted from greater JTTF collaboration, HUMINT, and intelligence analysis.

(U) Human Sources

(U) The FBI has a direct responsibility for identifying and preventing homeland attacks, as "no other Federal, state, or local program shares FBI's authorities and responsibilities for domestic intelligence collection."[105] Detecting both Homegrown Violent Extremists (HVEs) and operatives of a broader terrorist network operating on US soil given the difficulty of accessing their electronic communications, however, will increasingly require an effective HUMINT collection network. The Review Commission recognizes that the widespread availability of sophisticated online communications to conceal extremist activities, combined with rigorous legal requirements to obtain approval for collection techniques involving US persons in the United States, compound the difficulties faced by the FBI in identifying potential homeland terrorist threats.[106] The Review Commission determined that none of the five cases benefited from intelligence acquired through FBI recruited human sources.

(U) Post 9/11, the FBI's leadership recognized the FBI's unique role and in 2008 directed special agents with a HUMINT specialty to focus on developing long-term CHSs "with placement and access to strategic threat issues in support of critical national intelligence issues (such as the National Intelligence Priority Framework) or FBI Priorities (such as the TRP Band I–III threats)" rather than in support of cases.[107] Our visits to the field offices affirmed the importance of the FBI's HUMINT program, but raised serious questions regarding the lack of programmatic guidance from Headquarters and its uneven implementation in the field, which we address more fully in Chapter III.

(U) In January 2009, Najibullah Zazi moved from New York City (which is covered by the New York Field Office), to Aurora, Colorado (which is under the jurisdiction of the Denver Field Office). Neither FBI office was aware of Zazi or his associates before September 2009 when Zazi was preparing to travel to New York City to carry out the plot and after he had traveled to Pakistan and been trained by al-Qa'ida.[108] Neither the FBI nor local US law enforcement had acquired intelligence on Zazi's plot before a tip that originated outside the FBI triggered the investigation. Moreover, the FBI's outreach into the Afghan and Pakistani communities in

---

105 (U) Strategic Evaluation Report: FBI from a HUMINT Prospective January 2012, referenced in Scott McBride, "The Impact of HUMINT Squads on FBI's Collection Capabilities," *Senior Intelligence Officer Essay* (*McBride Essay*), August 22, 2013; (U) Memorandum for the Record, November 14, 2014.

106 (U) For more on the limits of domestic collection and how it impacts USIC collection posture against potential Homeland threats see: National Intelligence Council, *Terrorist Threats to the US Homeland 2016,* NIE 2013-08D (*Homeland NIE*), November 26, 2013:viii.

107 (U) *McBride Essay*, 2.

108 (U) Memorandum for the Record, July 28, 2014.; Memorandum for the Record, September 18, 2014.

Denver and New York did not result in a community member providing information or intelligence on Zazi or his associates.[109] Zazi's financial insolvency and his final preparations to procure enough hydrogen peroxide to make Tri-acetone Tri-peroxide did not rise to the FBI's attention.[110]

(U) Although HUMINT was not critical to raising Major Nidal Hasan to the attention of the FBI, tasking human sources to better understand Hasan's interactions with Anwar al-Aulaqi and his ultimate intentions would have been a prudent step for either the FBI or the Defense Criminal Investigative Service (DCIS). The FBI first learned of Major Hasan through an e-mail that he sent to the US-born radical cleric Anwar al-Aulaqi on December 17, 2008. Despite the fact that an active-duty US Army Major was e-mailing a known al-Qa'ida ideologue and facilitator who was the subject of an ongoing FBI investigation, the e-mail generated little concern in the context of what the Webster Commission termed a "crushing" volume of data.[111] While the purpose of the program was intended to be a "strategic intelligence collection platform" in order to generate intelligence regarding al-Aulaqi's location, movements, and contacts as a known al-Qa'ida radicalizer, the e-mails between Hasan and al-Aulaqi were not treated as serious intelligence leads.[112] Senior FBI officials involved in the case readily admitted that the Bureau needs to better understand the strategic component of preventing terrorist attacks, which the Review Commission believes requires more pro-active intelligence collection outside of case support.[113] One option available to the FBI, for instance, would have been to task its intelligence assets, including HUMINT, to develop the information further given the number of unknowns regarding the communications between Hasan and al-Aulaqi, for counterintelligence or counterterrorism purposes.[114] Accordingly, the Review Commission recommends accelerating the further development and refinement of an agile strategic intelligence program incorporating both HUMINT and domain awareness to identify individuals susceptible to being radicalized like Hasan, while preserving protections for First Amendment activities.

(U) Broader domain awareness, might have detected TTP plots in the United States and perhaps Faisal Shahzad would have been identified before his attempted plot to detonate a bomb. Shahzad, a Pakistani-born US citizen, had made multiple trips to Pakistan between 2007 and 2008 and had been radicalized by persons associated with the TTP, the group believed to have been behind the assassination of Benazir Bhutto in December 2007.[115] The FBI was aware of the potential homeland threat posed by the TTP, yet it is unclear to the Review Commission how many HUMINT squads or collection action plans were actively working to mitigate the potential threat in 2010.

---

109 (U) Ibid.; FBI Briefing, *Operation High Rise* (*High Rise Briefing*), April 1, 2014.
110 (U) Seth Jones, *Hunting in the Shadows: The Pursuit of Al-Qa'ida Since 9/11* (Hunting in the Shadows) (New York: W.W. Norton & Company, 2012): 322-326.
111 (U) *Webster Commission Report*, 35.; *A Ticking Time Bomb:* 38.
112 (U) *Webster Commission Report*, 35; Memorandum for the Record, February 19, 2014.
113 (U) Memorandum for the Record, October 1, 2014.
114 (U) Under the Federal Bureau of Investigation's Domestic Investigation and Operations Guide (DIOG) FBI employees are required to use the least intrusive means to investigate and analyze possible threats to national security. Federal Bureau of Investigation, *Domestic Investigations and Operations Guide,* §18.5.5.1, and § 5.6.3.1.8.1, October 23, 2014.
115 (U) Memorandum for the Record, September 2, 2014.

(U) In Boston, although Tamerlan Tsarnvaev's radicalization was known to some friends and colleagues, including at his mosque, the FBI did not understand the extent of his extremist views until after the bombings.[116] Russia's Federal Security Service (FSB) passed a lead to the FBI in March 2011 that Tamerlan Tsarnaev and his mother Zubeidat were followers of radical Islam and that Tamerlan intended "to travel to Russia to join unspecified 'bandit underground groups' in Dagestan and Chechnya."[117] The FBI opened but then closed an assessment on Tamerlan concerning his potential threat to national security, concluding on June 24, 2011, that he had "no link or nexus" to terrorism.[118] At the conclusion of the FBI's assessment, the FBI's findings were passed to Russian authorities via tear line with a request for specific information pertaining to Tamerlan Tsarnaev's alleged involvement in extremist activities. No response was ever received from Russian authorities. Given the limited information on Tamerlan, the FBI did not nominate him for inclusion on the Terror Watchlist. The Central Intelligence Agency (CIA), however, independently nominated Tamerlan for inclusion on the Terror Watchlist in October 2011—based on the same information lead from the Russians, which had been passed separately to the CIA the previous month.[119] The Inspectors General's report following the Boston Marathon bombing, which was provided to the Review Commission in April 2014, agreed that "there was insufficient derogatory information to establish reasonable suspicion that Tsarnaev was a known or suspected terrorist."[120]

(U) In November 2012, Tamerlan interrupted a sermon discussing Islamic and American holidays at the Islamic Society of Boston Cultural Center in Cambridge, but it does not appear that this information was ever reported to the FBI.[121] In January 2013, Tamerlan again became angry following a sermon at the same mosque.[122] This information does not appear to have made its way to the FBI. While the Review Commission recognizes the civil liberties sensitivities of source networks within religious institutions, a more extensive HUMINT network postured within the local community could have made the FBI aware of these outbursts. All of the cases revealed to the Review Commission that the FBI's role within the USIC as the primary collector of domestic human intelligence is of critical importance in the identification of potential threats.

(U) Intelligence Analysis and Domain Awareness

(U) In all five cases, when the FBI eventually became aware of the plotters, intelligence analysts played a critical role in the investigations. Still, in three of the five case studies, it was a tip from

---

116 (U) Inspectors General, *Unclassified Summary of Information Handling Prior to the Boston Marathon Bombings* (*IG Summary of Information Handling*), April 10, 2014: 1,2.
117 (U) Ibid., 8.
118 (U) Ibid., 8-10.
119 (U) Ibid., 11.
120 (U) Ibid.
121 (U) Associated Press, "Remembering the Tragedy: Timeline of Events in the Boston Marathon Bombing," *Huffington Post*, April 14, 2014, http://www.huffingtonpost.com/2014/04/14/boston-marathon-timeline_n_5145615.html (accessed December 11, 2014).
122 (U) Ibid.

outside the FBI that triggered the investigation.[123] In both the Hasan and Tsarnaev cases, while the FBI learned of the relevant individuals prior to the attack and conducted initial assessments, they were both closed prior to the Fort Hood shooting and Boston Marathon bombings after FBI agents concluded that none of the individuals in question warranted further investigation. Although a single analyst was spending 40 percent of his or her time reviewing al-Aulaqi's communications, intelligence analysts nonetheless played a minor role in the ultimate disposition of the Hasan and Tsarnaev assessments.[124] The Review Commission understands that the gravity and complexities of the Hasan and Tsarnaev plots were unclear, particularly given the lack of specific information alongside the high volume of competing and often uncertain threat information inundating FBI special agents and intelligence analysts. We do not intend to second guess the decision-making of dedicated special agents and intelligence analysts *ex post facto*. However, the cases raise concerns about how effectively the FBI empowers and equips its analysts to drive the intelligence cycle in the field and what contributions analysts with deep subject matter expertise might have added to those assessments.

(U) FBI intelligence programs in Denver and New York did not identify Zazi or his two main accomplices, Zarein Ahmedzay (who, like Zazi, was an Afghan born in a Pakistani refugee camp) and Adis Medunjanin (a native of Bosnia), in advance of the plot.[125] Zazi was unknown to local authorities, the FBI, or the USIC—despite the fact that he had traveled to Pakistan in 2008 where he had joined al-Qa'ida, been trained in bomb making at al-Qa'ida facilities in South Waziristan, and was in contact with such senior al-Qa'ida luminaries.[126] Back in the United States, Zazi was not subjected to secondary screening by Customs and Border Protection (CBP) at the airport and later in Colorado his separate purchases of 6 and 12 bottles of hydrogen peroxide, a key ingredient in the homemade bomb, went unreported to authorities.[127] The subsequent investigation revealed that Zazi had traveled to Pakistan on August 28, 2008, and returned to the United States on January 15, 2009.[128] Once the FBI learned of the connection between Zazi and the known AQ-affiliated e-mail account, full investigations and 24-hour surveillance were initiated on Zazi and subsequently his New York-based associates.[129]

(U) In the Headley and Shahzad cases, the plotters exhibited distinct travel and behavioral patterns that might have provided the broader USIC with advance warning of potentially suspicious activities if the data had been known to or aggregated by the FBI and other USIC analysts as part of a comprehensive domain awareness program. Headley had previously come to the attention of US law enforcement authorities, but FBI officials repeatedly concluded that Headley did not pose a threat at the time. He also came to the attention of US law enforcement authorities by way of accusations of violence and radicalism from family members, but FBI

---

123 (U) Zazi, Headley, and Tsarnaev.

124 (U) *Webster Commission Report,* 35. Additionally, the *IG Summary of Information Handling,* does not indicate analyst involvement in the FBI's final determination on Tsarnaev.

125 (U) Memorandum for the Record, July 28, 2014.; Memorandum for the Record, September 18, 2014.

126 (U) *High Rise Briefing.* See also Memorandum for the Record, April 1, 2014.; Hunting in the Shadows, 315-320.

127 (U) *Hunting in the Shadows,* 324-325.

128 (U) *Hunting in the Shadows,* 311, 323.

129 (U) *Hunting in the Shadows,* 326; Memorandum for the Record, July 28, 2014.; Memorandum for the Record, September 18, 2014.

officials repeatedly concluded that he did not pose a threat at the time. In December 2007, Headley's Moroccan wife complained to US officials at the US Embassy in Islamabad that her husband was a terrorist. The FBI investigation of Headley did not begin until 2009, and it was triggered by a tip that originated outside the FBI that revealed his relationships with extremists abroad.[130] One of the main lessons from the Headley case is that absent an intelligence effort across the USIC to understand the connections among cases and complaints across field offices, relevant intelligence may fall by the wayside. News outlets have reported, prior to his terrorist activities, Headley had worked as a DEA informant in the late 1990s and the early 2000s, following two heroin trafficking arrests.[131] A single complaint may be more easily dismissed as a poison pen motive, but several unrelated complaints should not be dismissed as readily as the work of a malcontent.

(U) Headley's Moroccan wife similarly complained to US officials at the US Embassy in Islamabad in December 2007 that her husband was a terrorist.[132] The Headley case raises the important question faced by all intelligence agencies—certainly important to the FBI—of how to scan and assess voluminous amounts of collected information strategically and identifying valuable intelligence leads. Still, more than a decade after 9/11, the FBI must prioritize empowering and equipping its analytic cadre to make these connections with cutting edge technology, to minimize the risk of the FBI missing important intelligence information.

(U) Hasan was not initially assessed as posing a terrorism threat, in large part because the full extent of his e-mail communications with al-Aulaqi were not comprehensively reviewed by the special agent and intelligence analyst in San Diego, thus missing the connection between Hasan's initial e-mail and his subsequent communications with al-Aulaqi.[133] Hasan, as a US military officer communicating with a senior al-Qa'ida facilitator, should certainly have been regarded as an intelligence—and potentially a counterintelligence—concern by the FBI.[134] As the Webster Commission Report points out, the al-Aulaqi e-mails were reviewed for pertinent foreign intelligence data and occasionally used to identify "previously unknown persons of potential interest through their contact with al-Aulaqi."[135] Determining if information from the al-Aulaqi intercept was of intelligence value fell to the San Diego intelligence analyst, whose mission was to disseminate "intelligence that has the potential to protect the US against threats to national security or improve the effectiveness of law enforcement."[136] In this instance, that responsibility was overridden by his case agent superior.

---

130 (U) FBI Briefing, April 2, 2014.

131 (U) Sebastian Rotella, "The American Behind India's 9/11—And How U.S. Botched Changes to Stop Him," *ProPublica*, January 24, 2014, http://www.propublica.org/article/david-headley-homegrown-terrorist (accessed December 11, 2014).

132 (U) Ibid.; Memorandum for the Record, September 2, 2014.; Memorandum for the Record, September 2, 2014.

133 (U) *Webster Commission Report, 46,47; A Ticking Time Bomb*, 38.

134 (U) Memorandum for the Record, February 19, 2014.; *A Ticking Time Bomb*, 10, 62.

135 (U) *Webster Commission Report,* 40.

136 (U) Ibid.; The FBI Intelligence Policy Manual, § 1.7; FBI Intelligence Information Report Handbook § 4.1.2; Privacy Impact Statement for the FBI, FBI Intelligence Information Report Dissemination Systems (FIDS) § 1.1, July 2, 2010.

(U) When Hasan's e-mail was first identified by the San Diego Field Office, the FBI special agent and intelligence analyst discussed the risk and value of producing an Intelligence Information Report (IIR) regarding Hasan's contact with al-Aulaqi.[137] According to the Webster Commission Report, the special agent decided erroneously in January 2009 that Hasan was a communications officer and therefore "might have access to IIRs and thus could learn about the intercept."[138] The desire to protect the program, based on an inaccurate interpretation of Hasan's military position, trumped the priority to disseminate the information. The Review Commission questions whether this decision should have been left to the special agent to determine based on our understanding of the FBI's existing intelligence policies at the time.[139] The incorrect assumptions made in the Hasan case highlight the potential benefit of a collaborative special agent-intelligence analyst relationship, where biases are routinely challenged and decision-making is more inclusive. The Review Commission is concerned that special agents be sensitive to the need of this inclusion when intelligence is prepared for dissemination to the USIC.[140] This should be addressed.

(U) The special agent assigned to investigate the Tsarnaevs did not consult any North Caucasus or counterterrorism subject-matter experts to understand the broader context and implications of the information provided by the FSB, although the Commision notes there was ample cause for skepticism. In April 2011, special agents interviewed both Tamerlan and his parents.[141] The special agents also spoke with Tamerlan in April.[142]

(U) A more thorough review of Tamerlan's activities by an intelligence analyst with the requisite subject matter expertise on terrorism and radicalization, working in collaboration with the special agent during the interview process, database searches, and subsequent evaluation of the information, may have led to a different interpretation of the significance of the FSB lead. The Inspector General's report on the Boston Marathon bombing noted that the special agents did not ask questions that were expected by their counterterrorism supervisor regarding Tamerlan's lifestyle and travel plans.[143] Moreover, the special agent did not contact the local Cambridge Police Department or complete a comprehensive search of all of baseline databases required in FBI's Baseline Collection Plan.[144] The Department of Justice's Office of the Inspector General concluded in the Boston case that "additional investigative steps would have resulted in a more thorough assessment," although it was impossible to know if these additional steps or searches would have yielded "additional information relevant to the FSB lead."[145]

---

137 (U) *Webster Commission Report*, 38, 45. According to the Webster report, "Dissemination of this information would have been appropriate, lawful, and consistent with FBI guidelines." *Webster Commission Report*, 74.
138 (U) *Webster Commission Report*, 44.
139 (U) Ibid.
140 (U) Memorandum for the Record, October 31, 2014.; Memorandum for the Record, November 14, 2014.; Memorandum for the Record, November 17, 2014.
141 (U) Inspectors General, *Review of Information Handling Prior to the April 15, 2012, Boston Marathon Bombings,* April 2014: 56-57.
142 (U) Ibid.
143 (U) Ibid., 61.
144 (U) Ibid., 50, 63.
145 (U) Ibid., 164.

(U) While Chechen terrorists have conducted multiple attacks over the years against Russian targets, they had never targeted the West, even after the 2007 declaration of the Imirat Kavkaz (Caucasian Emirate). The Boston Marathon investigation has shown that the Tsarnaevs, though of Chechen descent, were more likely HVEs. They were inspired by the global jihad, primarily through the lectures of Anwar al-Aulaqi and the jihadist publications of the online site Tibyan Publications. The Boston case demonstrates that the path to radicalization can be easily obscured from law enforcement. The proliferation of social media platforms and their continued exploitation by terrorist groups—and some of their media-savvy leaders—presents even more formidable challenges in tracking and identifying homegrown radicalization. Thus, successful detection is enhanced by the direct involvement of experienced intelligence analysts.

(U) In the Headley case, an analyst was ultimately able to connect him to an ongoing plot in Denmark, underscoring the value of good intelligence analysis in the field to meet the FBI's national security and investigative missions. While reviewing materials and information gathered during the investigation, FBI analysts and staff operations specialists (SOS) formulated a tentative theory that the threat posed by Headley was somehow related to the published cartoons of the Prophet Mohammed. An intelligence analyst on the Afghanistan/Pakistan squad noticed that one of the items included on an apparent operational checklist written by Headley were the words "Kings Square (French Embassy)."[146] The analysts determined that this referred to the location in Copenhagen of the the *Morgenavisen Jyllands-Posten* newspaper that had been the subject of numerous threats after publishing the cartoons. The analyst therefore concluded that Headley might be directly involved in a terrorist plot and alerted his superior.[147]

(U) After evaluating this case, it appears that Headley exhibited behavior that the FBI, in collaboration with the USIC, should have identified under its domain intelligence programs. The Review Commission strongly recommends that the Bureau must make it a high priority to further improve, refine, and strengthen its intelligence program. Additionally, in the Hasan and Tsarnaev cases, where the FBI had good information and solid leads pertaining to the plotters, the Review Commission believes that intelligence analysts should have participated in the questioning and evaluation of the information derived from the Tamerlan interview and the final assessment of the e-mails between Hasan and al-Aulaqi. It is heartening to note that a critic of the FBI's performance in these cases was especially complimentary in describing the new generation of special agents who have emerged since the September 2001 attacks and the FBI's willingness to collaborate across the USIC.[148]

(U) Communication, Collaboration, and Information Sharing Involving JTTFs

(U) Each field office involved in the five cases (Boston, Chicago, Denver, New York, San Diego, and Washington DC) had JTTFs supported by state, local, and other federal agency cooperation; community outreach; and on-going community engagement efforts. Indeed, although FBI tripwires were established nationwide, none of the individuals were involved in any overt illegal activities that warranted a local JTTF's full investigation. The FBI should work

---

146 (U) Memorandum for the Record, September 2, 2014.
147 (U) Memorandum for the Record, September 2, 2014.
148 (U) Memorandum for the Record, February 19, 2014.

to balance the JTTF's investigative role with the Bureau's intelligence and preventative mission. Accordingly, wherever possible the JTTF's information sharing structures should be better utilized to aggregate disparate intelligence information that might uncover a plot and prevent an attack.

(U) When Zazi and his co-conspirators left for Pakistan in August 2008, the three men were individually questioned by CBP officers, yet when Zazi returned to the United States in January 2009 he was not subjected to any secondary checks or additional screening.[149] The Review Commission's inquiries at the various field offices it visited confirmed that in this instance, there was no information to report to the Denver or New York JTTFs for further investigation.[150] We know now, through the benefit of hindsight, that Zazi did meet with known al-Qa'ida members in North and South Waziristan.[151]

(U) David Headley was an even more elusive target. He conducted his activities with all the skills of a trained intelligence operative—able to travel to and from the United States, Pakistan, and India with relative ease and eluding authorities.[152] The FBI had no knowledge of Headley's connections to LeT until provided with a tip that originated outside the FBI that prompted the investigetion in 2009. In 2007, when Headley's third wife complained regarding Headley's LeT connections to American embassy officials in Islamabad she was reportedly interviewed by the State Department and US Immigrations and Customs Enforcement, who relayed the information to the USIC.[153] This information was not passed to the FBI.[154]

(U) The Hasan case generally demonstrated poor coordination between JTTFs. Although there were no outward signs of illegal activity on Hasan's part from the outset, the FBI had enough information to establish at least a connection between the radical imam and the US Army officer. According to the Webster Commission report, the FBI had intercepted communications between al-Aulaqi and Hasan, who had e-mailed him from the DC metropolitan area.[155] The Washington Field Office's JTTF was passed a discretionary lead from San Diego, and the Hasan assessment was passed to the task force officer (TFO) from the DCIS. The DCIS officer concluded that

---

149 (U) Memorandum for the Record, September 18, 2014.; *High Rise Briefing.*

150 (U) Memorandum for the Record, April 1, 2014.; Memorandum for the Record, September 18, 2014.

151 (U) *Hunting in the Shadows*, 316-317. Upon inquiring into the Zazi matter, the Review Commission learned of the tension within the information sharing relationship between NYPD's Intelligence Division and the JTTF, particularly with regard to leaks of sensitive case-related information during pursuit of Zazi. (U) Memorandum for the Record September 17, 2014.; *Enemies Within*, 18-19; 123-125; 149-150.

152 (U) Memorandum for the Record, September 2, 2014.

153 (U) Sebastian Rotella, "The American Behind India's 9/11—And How U.S. Botched Changes to Stop Him," *ProPublica*, January 24, 2014, http://www.propublica.org/article/david-headley-homegrown-terrorist (accessed 11 December 2014); Memorandum for the Record, September 2, 2014.

154 (U) Ibid.

155 (U) The IP address Hasan used resolved to Northern Virginia, although his home and place of work were in Maryland. For the IP Address information see: *Webster Commission Report*, 44. For information on Hasan's work and residence see: Bob Drogin and Faye Fiore, "Retracing Steps of Suspected Fort Hood Shooter, Nidal Malik Hasan," *The Los Angeles Times*, November 7, 2009; Mary Pat Flaherty, William Wan, Derek Kravitz, and Christian Davenport, "Suspect, devout Muslim from Va. Wanted Army Discharge, Aunt Said, *The Washington Post*, November 6, 2009; Asha Beh and Jackie Bensen, "Fort Hood Shooting Suspect Was 'A Calm Person.'" *NBCWashington.com*, November 8, 2009.

Hasan's connection to al-Aulaqi was not improper and the assessment was closed. The San Diego JTTF requested follow-on interviews shortly thereafter, but the Washington Field Office declined. San Diego made two more requests for interviews, but Washington considered the matter resolved. San Diego did not pursue it either with the National JTTF or with FBI Headquarters.[156] In response to the Webster Commission report, the FBI eliminated discretionary leads, made a concerted effort to improve collaboration within and among JTTFs, established a formal process for sharing information relevant to military force protection with the National Joint Terrorism Task Force (NJTTF), and standardized database training for all JTTF TFOs.[157]

(U) In contrast to the Hasan case, the Times Square bombing case was a good example of positive JTTF collaboration with organizations external to the FBI. Shahzad displayed skill in evading detection by the JTTF in New York. He was technologically savvy, which enabled him to avoid detection on anyone's radar screen. [158] However, JTTF coordination after his botched bombing attempt demonstrated precisely just how well cooperation can work. The case against Shahzad did not begin pursuant to any tip, lead, or JTTF informant; rather street vendors spotted smoke coming from the faulty explosive device inside his vehicle and contacted authorities. This time, armed with the knowledge and best practices learned from the Zazi experience, the JTTF with NYPD were able to identify Shahzad within 48 hours.[159]

(U) The Review Commission emphasizes here that a further clarification of the mutual responsibilities of the Task Force members and the FBI on JTTFs is essential. While the FBI institutionalized information sharing procedures on counterterrorism investigations that may pose a risk to the Department of Defense, similar formal procedures governing JTTF information sharing could benefit other important US Government, state, and local relationships. Additionally, the composition of JTTFs across the country—though currently up to the discretion of the respective Special Agent in Charge (SAC)—could adhere to a more standardized structure to ensure key partners are included. Moreover, if particular departments cannot afford to have full-time personnel assigned to the JTTF, a structure creating designated touch points in the department whom the JTTF can contact may improve collaboration. JTTF information sharing relationships is addressed more comprehensively in Chapter IV.

(U) Counterterrorism Legal Authorities

(U) The legal authorities afforded by the Electronic Communications Privacy Act (ECPA), Foreign Intelligence Surveillance Act (FISA), and USA PATRIOT Act, as well as Communications Assistance for Law Enforcement Act (CALEA) mandate for specific communication companies, were crucial to the FBI in investigating all five cases. The results in these cases highlight the importance of maintaining sufficient legal authorities to conduct counterterrorism investigations. FISAs, including 702 authorizations, and National Security

---

156 (U) *Webster Commission Report,* 58-60.
157 (U) Electronic Communication, August 2, 2011.
158 (U) Memorandum for the Record, September 18, 2014.
159 (U) Memorandum for the Record, September 17, 2014.; Memorandum for the Record, September 19, 2014.

Letters (NSLs) were particularly helpful. The monitoring, preservation, and upgrading of these laws is essential to enable the FBI to keep pace with the evolving terrorist threat.

(U) In the Zazi case, when he drove from Denver to New York, the FBI obtained a warrant for his laptop and continued to monitor his communications.[160] Upon analyzing Zazi's computer, FBI special agents discovered his notes regarding building a homemade bomb that were derived from the training he received at al-Qa'ida facilities in Pakistan. Without this evidence, the case against Zazi would have been difficult to prove.[161] Moreover, Zazi's willingness to provide a detailed statement to the FBI was due, in part, to the FBI's possession of his notes on bomb-making.[162]

(U) In Chicago, NSLs helped the FBI track David Headley and better understand his involvement in the Copenhagen plot directed by Ilyas Kashmiri, al-Qa'ida's chief of external operations at the time and the head of the Pakistani extremist organization, Harakat ul Jihad al Islami.[163] Over the next several months, the FBI obtained warrants on Headley and on his associate Rana. Based on the information obtained, FBI special agents decided to arrest Headley before he could leave the country.[164]

(U) In the Fort Hood shooting, surveillance on al-Aulaqi was critical in identifying Nidal Hasan. All of al-Aulaqi's incoming and outgoing communications had to be reviewed for two purposes: their intelligence value and to identify suspects who might commit terrorist acts. The FBI's al-Aulaqi team was tasked with reading and marking each communication as either "pertinent" or "non-pertinent" in the Data Warehouse System-Electronic Surveillance Data Management System, a system that stored information with controlled access.[165] Pertinent communications were deemed to contain evidence of a crime or foreign intelligence information.[166] Not surprisingly, this system produced a staggering amount of information, all of which required review and cataloguing by the al-Aulaqi team.[167] Moreover, in May 2008, al-Aulaqi had created a link on his website that allowed visitors to "Contact the Sheikh." It quickly attracted a large number of followers who sought religious advice and justification for their radicalization and/or intended violent acts.[168] Indeed, this new source of communication both greatly increased the al-Aulaqi team's workload. The legacy of al-Aulaqi's on-line communication has continued to radicalize Americans and many others throughout the world even after his death.

---

160 (U) Ibid.
161 (U) Ibid.; Memorandum for the Record, September 18, 2014.
162 (U) Ibid.
163 (U) Memorandum for the Record, September 2, 2014.
164 (U) Memorandum for the Record, September 2, 2014.
165 (U) *Webster Commission Report*, 37.
166 (U) *Webster Commission Report*, 38.
167 (U) *Webster Commission Report*, 35-37.
168 (U) *Webster Commission Report*, 35, 100.

(U) Anwar al-Aulaqi and the Age of Internet Radicalization

(U) In four of the five cases (Zazi, Shahzad, Hasan, and the Tsarnaevs), the Internet presence of now-deceased US born radical cleric Anwar al-Aulaqi provided some of the motivation and inspiration for the plotters' attacks.[169] Al-Aulaqi was a driving force behind the creation of widely accessible English-language Salafi-jihadist propaganda embodied through his own website (2008) and al-Qa'ida in the Arabian Peninsula's (AQAP) English-language *Inspire* magazine (2010), which spurred a new wave of Internet radicalization post 9/11.[170] In the years since, al-Aulaqi's media partly motivated at least 52 persons to participate in terrorist activities who were later indicted on terrorism-related charges.[171]

(U) Zazi, Shahzad, and Hasan engaged in their attack plotting prior to the release of *Inspire* and had accessed the radical cleric's statements online, while the Tsarnaevs were motivated in part by *Inspire* magazine's first issue–which provided the recipe for the pressure cooker bombs used in the attack. As the Boston Marathon bombings demonstrated, al-Qa'ida's ideology has outlived both Usama bin Laden and al-Aulaqi, partially fueled by the growth of terrorist chat rooms and social media applications that enable the spread of violent extremist propaganda and facilitate radicalization within the US.

(U) The 2011 death of al-Aulaqi stalled but did not prevent further spread of al-Qa'ida affiliated English-language media, as demonstrated by the 2014 launch of core al-Qa'ida's *Resurgence* magazine, AQAP's publication *Palestine: Betrayal of the Guilty Conscience*, and the Islamic State of Iraq and the Levant's magazine *Dabiq*. These publications, along with a growing body of English-language jihadist Tweets, videos, and online discussion forums, demonstrate al-Aulaqi's assertion: "The Internet has become a great medium for spreading the call of Jihad and following the news of the mujahideen."[172] The FBI must now contend with a threat environment where a speech, comment, Tweet, or video can travel around the world in seconds to facilitate radicalization—in one's own language and in the comfort of their home—and direct violence against the US. The age of Internet radicalization poses an unprecedented challenge, as the private and customized nature of this propaganda transcends geographic boundaries and demographics, impelling continuous innovation for the FBI. The proximity of such communications to otherwise protected First Amendment activity increases this challenge.

(U) In these and the other cases, available legal authorities were essential. In the Zazi and Headley cases, they helped the FBI gather intelligence and better understand the conspirators, possible targets, and key elements of the plot. In the Shahzad and Tsarnaev cases, the legal authorities were indispensable to identifying the conspirators after the respective attacks.

---

169 (U) For more on al-Aulaqi's influence over Zazi, Shahzad, and Hasan, see *Hunting in the Shadows*. It is important to note that al-Aulaqi was not the sole radicalizing influence on any of these individuals, many of whom also cited the teachings of radical cleric Shaykh Abdallah Ibrahim al-Faisal, among others.

170 (U) Al-Aulaqi helped create and edit *Inspire* along with Samir Khan, another now-deceased radicalized US citizen who was the other driving force behind Inspire magazine. For more on Samir Khan see: Robbie Brown and Kim Severson "Second American in Strike Waged Qaeda Media War" *The New York Times*, September 30, 2011. Additionally, at least 16 of the U.S. persons indicted since 2010 cited *Inspire* magazine as a direct influence. Peter Bergen and David Sterman, "The Man Who Inspired the Boston Bombings" CNN.com, April 11, 2014.

171 (U) Peter Bergen and David Sterman, "The Man Who Inspired the Boston Bombings," CNN.com, April 11, 2014.

172 (U) *Hunting in the Shadows*, 341. Quote originally appeared in Anwar al-Aulaqi's February 2009 *Inspire* article "44 Ways to Support Jihad."

Ultimately, even in the Hasan case, the FBI identified him using these legal authorities, but then failed to comprehend the gravity of his communications with al-Aulaqi.

(U) Findings and Recommendations

(U) The cases examined provided the focus for the findings and recommendations contained in Chapters III and IV.

CHAPTER III
(U) ANTICIPATING NEW THREATS AND MISSIONS

(U) In the future, the FBI will be challenged by a complex threat environment that will require greater agility, deeper integration across the United States government (USG), and better strategic as well as tactical intelligence. From foreign fighters in Syria and Iraq to potentially crippling cyber attacks, the FBI must be prepared to respond to a diverse array of threats originating from inside the United States and abroad. There will be no pause, as nation states and non-state actors endeavor to find ways to make it increasingly difficult for the FBI to identify, understand, and mitigate these threats. At the same time, the fiscal environment is likely to make the FBI's ability to execute its mission even harder, as will threats of unauthorized disclosures of classified information that could degrade intelligence missions.[173] Chapter III discusses how the FBI has positioned itself to address new and emerging threats:

(U) Key Points

- (U) The FBI division-level strategic plans are useful as management tools, but they are not uniformly threat-based nor do they align with a needed corporate strategic plan for the Bureau that would allocate resources against current and emerging national security threats.

- (U) The Bureau's Threat Review and Prioritization (TRP) process improves FBI's ability to track and manage progress against existing threats; it connects FBI Headquarters' priorities to the field offices' strategies to mitigate threats. However, it does not look beyond the current-year time horizon.

- (U) In order to effectively address the evolving threat environment, the FBI should continue to enhance and invest in the intelligence analyst workforce. Additionally, the FBI should strive to further clarify human intelligence (HUMINT) guidance at the Headquarters level and more clearly define and develop domain analysis, a cornerstone of FBI threat analysis and intelligence production.

- (U) FBI threat assessments, as captured in the Consolidated Strategy Guide (CSG), should be developed to align with long-term United States Intelligence Community (USIC) forecasts, which can and should inform FBI strategic planning.

(U) The Review Commission understands that the FBI addresses current and emerging threats on multiple levels: Headquarters' divisions, field offices, as well as through its legal attachés LEGATs. The FBI also participates with the wider USIC in a series of processes to identify these threats. The Review Commission, therefore, undertook a significant effort to examine all relevant aspects of the FBI national security mission.[174] At the enterprise level, the FBI uses its strategic focus areas and strategy map to guide the FBI's strategic direction. The FBI strategy map is cascaded down to the divisions in an effort to ensure that the strategies executed by the individual divisions are in line with overall organizational strategic goals. According to the FBI, the strategy is monitored on a routine basis through quarterly strategy reviews which are

---

173 (U) Director of National Intelligence, *The National Intelligence Strategy of the United States of America*, 2014, 4.

174 (U) Note: This report does ***not address*** the counterintelligence mission.

conducted first at the division level and then at the Director level. All headquarters divisions have their own multi-year strategic plans which the Review Commission undertook to examine in depth.

(U) Strengthening the Intelligence Workforce

(U) The Intelligence Branch (IB) is responsible for the career development of the FBI's intelligence personnel. These personnel work in partnership with special agents, within the operational divisions and field offices, to design and execute strategies against current and emerging threats. This structure is not unlike the US military, in which the Armed Services train and equip soldiers, sailors and airmen, while the combatant commands execute US national security strategy. Because the professional analytic staff of the FBI underpins the process by which the FBI prioritizes threats, the Review Commission examined IB programs pertaining to the development of its Strategic Plan and its Program of Analysis (POA) as well as to the professionalization of the workforce. The findings from that effort are summarized below. Subsequent sections turn to our review of FBI strategies to mitigate current and emerging threats.

(U) *Strategic Plan and Program of Analysis*

(U) The IB's Strategic Plan articulates in broad terms the objectives of the FBI's intelligence program, rather than providing a blueprint for allocating resources against specific threats. As such, it is best understood as a guide to enhancing an intelligence capability for the FBI through a process of programmatic objectives. The strategy addresses six categories of objectives spread out over a five-year period (2014-2018): workforce success, culture and mindset, technology capabilities, collection, information sharing, and exploitation and analysis.[175]

(U) The Review Commission believes that the IB's strategic plan falls short in several key respects. First, we observed that the objectives laid out in the IB's strategy seem more in line with a newly established organization. For example, the strategy does not anticipate that the FBI will have "broken down the cultural barrier between Special Agents and Intelligence Analysts" until 2017.[176] Second, the strategy appears to lack context and urgency—making only passing reference to the increasingly complex set of threats and issues the FBI will face in the future and not identifying them as critical drivers for change. Third, and finally, the Review Commission found it surprising that the strategy—while correctly noting the important contribution, for example, of Geospatial Intelligence—makes little mention of building a capability to produce strategic, all-source intelligence assessments that will guide planning and inform resource decisions and help the FBI to anticipate tomorrow's threats. The IB recently revised the Intelligence Program Policy Guide which provides direction to this end.[177]

---

175 (U) Federal Bureau of Investigation, *Leading the Way: Federal Bureau of Investigation Intelligence Strategy 2014-2018*: 3.
176 (U) Ibid., 5.
177 (U) Ibid., 14.

54

(U) Despite our concerns with the IB Strategic Plan, the Review Commission found that the POA for FY15 reflects what one might expect of a strategic plan for an intelligence program.[178] Organized by divisional programs and missions, threat bands, and key intelligence questions, this POA is impressive in its breadth of coverage. The Review Commission believes that, taken together, the strategic plan and POA are on the right path forward. We remain concerned, however, that this current path will not produce the enhanced subject matter expertise in a meaningful timeframe for the FBI to address emerging threats.

(U) Professionalization of the Workforce

(U) Most of the Review Commission's concerns revolve around the need to further professionalize the intelligence workforce. Beginning in 2005, the FBI re-aligned its intelligence and law enforcement missions and re-invented itself into a threat-based organization. It tripled the size of its intelligence workforce and created specific career tracks for intelligence personnel, including a separate track for staff operations specialists (SOSs).[179] This represents a tremendous effort. But the Review Commission believes that the FBI is missing a wholly professionalized workforce that has the available instruments to counter the threats facing the United States.

(U) In this context, the IB updated its Intelligence Analyst Developmental Plan in the spring of 2013.[180] Still, the Review Commission believes that the plan sufficiently addresses general intelligence tradecraft, but gives short shrift to the level and type of subject matter expertise and experience required to build such a program. To close this gap, we urge the FBI to increase opportunities for sabbaticals and academic training, detail assignments to other agencies, temporary overseas duty tours, and outreach to scholars on core national security issues. The purpose of these trainings and assignment opportunities is to facilitate innovative thinking and, therefore, better enable the FBI's intelligence analysts (IAs) to identify emerging threats.

(U) The Review Commission observed in its field office visits that there is confusion regarding the respective roles of SOS and intelligence analysts with SOSs sometimes performing intelligence analyst work and analysts performing traditional SOS tasks.[181] The deployment of several hundred SOSs in the last year to field operational squads intended to clarify the IA and SOS work roles but the Review Commission believes that sustained management attention will be required to resolve this confusion over time. The Review Commission learned that the SOS career field was conceived initially as a springboard to either special agent or intelligence analyst positions but over time this vision has become obscured and the career path of SOSs uncertain.[182] The Review Commission recommends that the FBI provide SOSs with clear and consistent

---

178 (U) Federal Bureau of Investigation, *Program of Analysis FY2015.*
179 (U) Staff operations specialists fill an important role in FBI investigations and case management. Special agents depend on SOS analytic capabilities to produce written products, compile discovery packages, build spreadsheets, and mine databases for tactical case support.
180 (U) Federal Bureau of Investigation, *Intelligence Analyst Developmental Plan,* May 2014.
181 (U) In some instances this was due to a shortage of intelligence analysts at the field offices. Memorandum for the Record, June 13, 2014.; Memorandum for the Record, August 14, 2014.; Memorandum for the Record, August 15, 2014.; Memorandum for the Record, August 18, 2014.
182 (U) Memorandum for the Record, June 18, 2014.

managerial guidance and produce unambiguous career path guidance that allows for transition into other professional roles.[183]

(U) Finally, the Review Commission strongly supports the attention of FBI senior leadership to elevate intelligence analysts to senior leadership positions in the IB.[184] We also believe that a greater proportion of the IB organization should be staffed with intelligence professionals, and that the IB should better leverage the wider USIC to help develop a customized FBI version of strategic analysis tradecraft. If the IB's purpose is to provide oversight, strategic direction, and support to the FBI's intelligence program, the Review Commission is convinced career intelligence officers should be entrusted with this responsibility to a greater extent.

(U) Accounting for New and Emerging Threats

(U) While the IB prepares the intelligence workforce, the operational divisions and field offices are responsible for the actual design and implementation of FBI strategies to respond to threats against the Homeland. The FBI primarily accounts for these current and emerging threats through its TRP process. Further, the operational divisions in FBI Headquarters develop overarching strategic plans that articulate their priorities over a five year period. The field offices also produce their own strategic plans and are responsible for mitigating threats in their areas of responsibility (AOR). The Review Commission, therefore, undertook a significant effort to examine the TRP, operational divisions' strategic plans, and field office efforts to mitigate new and emerging terrorist threats.

(U) *Threat Review and Prioritization (TRP) Process*

(U) Adopted by FBI Headquarters in fiscal year FY13, the TRP, and its accompanying Consolidated Strategy Guide (CSG), requires operational divisions and field offices to identify and prioritize national threat issues, develop mitigation strategies to counter these threats, and allocate resources accordingly. This process occurs on an annual basis. The benefit of the TRP is that it allows FBI headquarters to compare one field office's priorities—and resource allocation—with another field office and, at least theoretically, identify if gaps exist. To do this, the TRP utilizes a series of "threat bands" ranked I, II, III, IV, and so on.

(U) A series of Threat Mitigation Teams (TMTs) support the TRP process. TMTs are designed to help Field Intelligence Groups and operational squads collaborate on high priority threats identified in the TRP and CSG.[185] National Threat Priorities, or Band I threats, require field offices to establish a TMT for each. Band II contains local threat priorities and while TMTs are also required for this category of threats, field offices can determine within the TMT whether a threat relates to their specific geographic region or not. If not, the field office is required to

---

183 (U) The Review Commission understands that the Executive Assistant Director (EAD)/I will shortly provide SOSs a career development plan. Memorandum for the Record, August 18, 2014.
184 (U) "Message from Director Comey," August 5, 2014.
185 (U) Federal Bureau of Investigation, *Threat Review and Prioritization Process: Field Standard Operation Procedures*, May 27, 2013.; Memorandum for the Record, August 21, 2014.; Memorandum for the Record, August 15, 2014.

justify its decision to FBI Headquarters and, pending approval, can disband the TMT. Band III and Band IV threats are also addressed by FBI field offices. But, given their standing within the TRP and CSG, they are unlikely to receive as high a prioritization.

(U) Generally speaking, the Review Commission found that TRP processes handle current threats fairly well. Emerging threats, however, receive little emphasis in the TRP. In fact, the Review Commission was often told that acting on the threats not identified in the top bands would harm performance ratings.[186] This observation became evident as a result of extensive interviews conducted with special agents and intelligence analysts and their supervisors in the National Security Branch (NSB), the IB, and the Cyber Division (CYD), as well as at FBI field offices.

(U) The Syrian Foreign Fighter issue is a good example of the current limitations of the TRP process. The Review Commission believes that the FBI should have better postured its intelligence collection to get ahead of the changing developments within Syria and Iraq that gave rise to ISIL's growing strength and greater instability throughout the region. Other members of the USIC did so. The TRP process, while effectively addressing threats, does not provide a mechanism for the FBI divisions or field offices to proactively identify emerging threats based on their domain awareness. Nor is the TRP flexible enough to drive the prioritization of these threats once they are identified by the interagency coordination process. The Review Commission gives credit to the FBI's Counterterrorism Division (CTD) Middle East Fusion Cell for its efforts to marshal a response within the FBI to the dynamic and growing foreign-fighter threat. The Review Commission believes that the number of unanswered intelligence questions regarding foreign fighters, combined with the level of risk that they present to the Homeland should have afforded this threat higher prioritization under the TRPs and CSGs.

(U) It is thus clear to the Review Commission that the TRP process underemphasizes critical, over-the-horizon, threats. In an attempt to remedy this, the FBI initiated a new Warning and Anticipatory Intelligence Initiative (WAII) in the Spring of 2014, led by the IB's Strategic Issues Group which houses the Senior National Intelligence Officers (SNIOs), to identify over the horizon threats. This initiative was not mentioned by analysts during our field office visits. We believe that this shortfall can be attributed partly to the fact that the TRP process occurs annually with mid-year updates through the TMTs. The FBI's strategic plans, in contrast, articulate the operational divisions' and field offices' priorities over a multi-year period. The Review Commission accordingly examined these strategic plans to better understand how the FBI attempts to take into account emerging threats.

(U) *Counterterrorism Division Strategic Plan*

(U) **Division Focus.** The current CTD Strategic Plan states that the FBI's top priority since September 11, 2001, is to protect the US Homeland from another terrorist attack.[187] The strategic plan attempts to fulfill this mission through 10 specialized sections, including communications, terrorist financing, international terrorist operations, domestic terrorism and

---

186 (U) Memorandum for the Record, July 28, 2014.; Memorandum for the Record, August 12, 2014.
187 (U) Federal Bureau of Investigation, *FBI Counterterrorism Strategic Plan, 2012-2016*, October 2011: 4.

strategic operations. Its purpose is to respond to and anticipate the "ever changing dimensions" of threats five years into the future.[188] In addition, CTD uses its strategic shifts and strategy map to manage its overall division strategy. The shifts and the map are then cascaded to the field through the strategic guidance provided in CTD's chapter of the CSG.

(U) Emerging Threats. The CTD uses the TRP and its associated TMTs to identify emerging trends and to sensitize the field offices to these trends.[189] The analysts of CTD's intelligence branch look beyond the TRP to identify patterns and trends, an effort that needs to be expanded and strengthened in the view of the Review Commission. The CTD is not always aware of how thoroughly the field offices are carrying out specific counterterrorism tasks.[190] This suggests that the TRP alone is not an effective mechanism to coordinate between FBI divisions and field offices. More troubling, the Review Commission also discovered that CTD resources have been shifted frequently from "over the horizon threats" to immediate crises.[191] While understandable in a resource-constrained environment, CTD's approach also underemphasizes new and potential threats.

(U) Importantly, these two overarching challenges—underutilization of available tools to gain visibility into the field office's activities and limited resources devoted to emerging threats—surfaced repeatedly throughout the Review Commission's review of the divisions' strategic plans. They are not unique to CTD. We found some divisions have attempted to overcome these challenges through creative workarounds while others have not. Nonetheless, the systemic problems of both lack of transparency between Headquarters and field offices on emerging threats and scarce resources devoted to emerging threats were readily apparent to the Review Commission.

(U) Integration. The Review Commission found that CTD also falls short with respect to division-level integration of its strategic plan. Our interviews with CTD officials revealed that the division does not believe cross-pollination occurs regularly between the strategic plans.[192] Logically speaking, increasing division resources to identify emerging threats may not be enough if these resources are not distributed where they are the most needed. For example, should more resources be devoted to cyber threats from organized crime or to threats from Syrian foreign fighters? Or, with respect to support functions, should the FBI hire more cyber experts or personnel to undertake human intelligence collection? It is difficult to fully understand these tradeoffs without some degree of cross-pollination or integration across division-level strategic plans.

(U) Further, a number of field offices complained to the Review Commission regarding the lack of a single point of contact at CTD.[193] The field offices also believe that CTD officials are

---

188 (U) *Counterterrorism Strategic Plan, 2012-2016*: 1.
189 (U) Memorandum for the Record, October 21, 2014.
190 (U) Ibid.
191 (U) Ibid.
192 (U) Ibid.
193 (U) Memorandum for the Record, September 19, 2014;; Memorandum for the Record, August 14, 2014.

58

reluctant to empower field office subject matter expertise on counterterrorism cases.[194] Part of this disconnect may simply be the result of CTD's basic structure: the International Terrorist Organizations Section I (ITOS I) and Section II (ITOS II) within the FBI's CTD are organized geographically, rather than by threat. CTD officials were forthright regarding internal debates on geographic versus threat-based structures. It is clear to the Review Commission that CTD has considered the advantages and disadvantages of both approaches and hence chose to organize ITOS I and II by region.[195] The Review Commission does not feel able to recommend that CTD reorganize ITOS I and II. Instead, a more consistent point of contact should be designated within CTD for the field offices with respect to current and, especially, emerging threats. The Review Commission also recommends that CTD reexamine the possibility of a transition to a threats-based organizational structure in the near future.

(U) Other Observations. Finally, CTD representatives also acknowledged in our interviews that their strategic plan did not drive resource allocation. Instead, the leadership cited the FBI's Time Utilization and Record Keeping system (TURK) and the case classification and Crime Problem Indicator (CPI) codes as the means by which the division retroactively determined how special agents and intelligence analysts accounted for their time.[196] There is no similar forward looking system to determine personnel assignment priorities based on the threat or intelligence picture. The CTD strategic plan should drive resource allocation for the counterterrorism mission.

(U) *Cyber Division Strategic Plan*

(U) Division Focus. The Review Commission found that the CYD's Strategic Plan is not organized around specific threats, but instead focuses on supporting the needs of subject matter experts in the field offices. In this context, CYD's strategic plan is very different in intent from CTD. CYD has five primary lines of operation: outreach and information sharing, operations, intelligence, workforce development, and technology. CYD uses the TRP to inform field office prioritization against specific cyber intrusion sets and a Cyber Threat Team (CTT) model drives strategies based on the highest-priority specific threats.[197]

(U) Addressing the cyber threat presents unique challenges to an organization where most operational activity occurs in field offices with clearly defined geographic AOR. The cyber threat does not, however, respect geographic boundaries. Often the only connection a cyber incident has to a particular field office is the presence of a victim in its AOR. CYD recently re-organized and adopted the CTT model that is structured according to cyber intrusion sets. The CTT model was designed, among other reasons, to overcome the previously identified lack of strategic coordination among and between the field offices on cyber national security threats, to integrate field resources with the USIC, and to fully leverage FBI cyber resources. The CTT model allows for dynamic reallocation of resources, as necessary, in a virtual operational environment. The CTTs address this problem by establishing a formal coordination mechanism

---

194 (U) Ibid.
195 (U) Memorandum for the Record, October 21, 2014.
196 (U) Ibid.
197 (U) Memorandum for the Record, October 2, 2014.

between the field offices and Headquarters.[198] The model assigns a primary strategic field office and collaborative tactical field offices for specific prioritized cyber national security intrusion sets. This is an effort to reduce the amount of duplication where multiple field offices expend resources to monitor the same intrusion sets, including ones that originate overseas.[199] And, then, CYD also has a dedicated support element at FBI Headquarters. It is difficult to determine exactly how effective this CYD structure will be, as it is a relatively recent development, but it appears to have resolved the primary complaint by field offices regarding the lack of a single point of contact.

(U) Emerging Threats. In our interviews, CYD staff credited the TRP as a relatively effective management tool to coordinate FBI efforts against specific cyber intrusion sets. CYD staff also took advantage of opportunities within the TRP to submit "write-in" candidates relevant to cyber threats. Yet, in those same interviews, CYD staff also conceded that once resources are allocated under the annual TRP, the division had to scramble to reallocate existing resources to address any newly-identified threat or intrusion-set. This challenge was not unique to CYD but surfaced repeatedly throughout our interviews.[200] The Review Commission views this as problematic: it discourages anticipatory or preemptive actions and it may even degrade ongoing activities against high-priority threats. To achieve a high performing rating.

(U) Integration. The Review Commission also learned that CYD remains underfunded and continues to struggle with the recruitment of personnel with the requisite advanced computer science skills.[201] The skill-sets required for the CYD mission are unique. Accordingly, the Review Commission strongly believes that pressing national security and operational requirements exist in this specific area of the FBI's national security and criminal remits.[202] If CYD's strategic plan is not integrated into a wider FBI strategy, the Review Commission fears that it will be more challenging for the FBI's senior leadership to understand the tradeoffs in, for example, hiring for certain types of skill sets, e.g. computer scientists, versus other categories of prioritized expertise. An integrated FBI strategy would more systemically prioritize FBI support functions, including human resources, with the objective of aligning critical support requirements to the highest priority missions.

---

198 (U) Ibid.

199 (U) The Review Commission was informed the CYD had considered a virtual field office to lead and coordinate the FBI's response to the cyber threat but rejected it as too inconsistent with the field office concept. Ordinarily events occurring overseas would be addressed by the extraterritorial squad in a field office with responsibility for the particular location. This construct is also imperfect in the cyber realm where the attack may emanate from a not always immediately known particular location and affect victims in multiple locations that are the responsibility of disparate field offices. Memorandum for Record, August 15, 2014,; Memorandum for Record, October 2, 2014.

200 (U) *Cyber Division,* Cyber Strategic Planning Briefing, October 2, 2014.

201 (U) For example, during a meeting with CYD leadership, it was estimated that as many as 27 FBI field offices are under-staffed. Readers should note, however, that CYD has lower attrition rates than CTD, WMD, and the IB across the board, for special agents, intelligence analysts and professional staff. The one exception is intelligence analysts: WMDD has a 2.9% attrition rate versus 3.3% for CYD. Response to Request for Information, *Attrition Rates by Selected Divisions/Personnel Type FY 2014*, November 12, 2014.

202 (U) CYD was keenly aware that they represented a mere 1/15 of the total FBI workforce and 1/35 of the FBI special agent workforce and therefore constantly had to defend FBI's need for specialized cyber skills within their own organization. Memorandum for the Record, October 2, 2014.

(U) Threat Examination and Scoping (TExAS) Tool

(U) The Cyber Division, and its Cyber threat team, must prioritize their efforts against potentially hundreds of intrusion sets. Equally challenging, given the nature of the cyber threat, these intrusion sets cross geographic boundaries and can alter or adapt quickly. So the Review Commission was particularly interested in learning more about a relatively new "TExAS Tool" that CYD developed to prioritize current threats and anticipate emerging threats.

(U) The TExAS tool was developed in the Spring of 2014 and implemented in June 2014. This innovative software signals the CTT's degree of confidence in its assessments. The data visualization tool also allows decision makers to prioritize or otherwise allocate resources toward new intrusions sets or towards ones where better intelligence is needed. The Review Commission commends CYD for developing the TExAS Tool. It may be a best practice for other division to consider

(U) *Weapons of Mass Destruction Directorate Strategic Plan*

(U) **Division Focus.** The overarching goal of the Weapons of Mass Destruction Directorate's (WMDD) 2015-2020 Strategic Plan is to leverage integrated intelligence and operational capabilities to work closely with domestic and international government and private partners to prevent and neutralize weapons of mass destruction (WMD) threats. A key objective is to "systematically identify novel or emerging science and technology with potential WMD applications."[203] The other nine objectives address being threat-focused and requirements driven; leveraging outreach to develop actionable intelligence; having intelligence-driven investigations; and leading the FBI and USG in WMD operational response. Consistent with the other operational divisions, however, the Review Commission found the WMDD strategic plan assumes unlimited resources and, therefore, only prioritizes resources annually under TRP.[204]

(U) Somewhat unique to this division, prevention and outreach are closely linked within its strategic plan. For example, through the auspices of its countermeasures program, the WMDD has developed relationships with the Association of American Scientists and partnerships with leading academic institutions.[205] The purpose of these relationships is to help the FBI identify and mitigate emerging WMD-related threats. During the course of our interviews, the Review Commission was provided with the Biological Countermeasures Program as an example of a "best practice" in this context.

(U) In July 2014, the FBI rapidly responded to secure previously undocumented vials of variola virus (smallpox) at the Bethesda-based National Institutes of Health. Though the resulting investigation proved there was no criminal intent, the incident appears to have sensitized other government agencies to the potential that unsecured biological materials in their offices may

---

203 (U) Federal Bureau of Investigation. *Strategic Plan 2015-2020: Weapons of Mass Destruction Directorate,* Weapons of Mass Destruction Directorate.
204 (U) Memorandum for Record, September 25, 2014.
205 (U) Ibid.

exist and precautions should be taken. The WMDD pointed to this event as indicative of its effective and timely identification of an emerging threat.[206]

(U) Emerging Threats. The WMDD's strategic plan does indeed emphasize emerging threats and technologies beyond the TRP. To maintain this focus, the WMDD has four dedicated fusion cells divided into specific modalities: chemical, biological, nuclear/radiological, and critical infrastructure.[207] The purpose of these fusion cells is to identify and track emerging threats within each discipline[208] The Review Commission believes this structure is well positioned to encourage and sustain efforts against new threats.

(U) Interestingly, the Review Commission understands the WMDD actually uses its fusion cells to augment the TRP in order to address emerging as well as current threats. That is, due to scarce resources, the WMDD uses the TRP threat banding to allocate fusion cell resources, including to address emerging threats, and makes adjustments throughout the year as needed. The WMDD's application of the TRP is thus more flexible than other divisions the Review Commission observed.

(U) Integration. WMDD representatives interviewed by the Review Commission believed that WMDD worked to cross-pollinate its strategic plan with others within the National Security Branch. Moreover, the WMDD's Global Terrorism Unit reported that input from WMDD's threat mitigation teams influenced the CTD's threat banding in FY14.[209] Intelligence analysis produced by WMDD's Proliferation Unit influenced CD's threat banding in FY14 by addressing the WMD portion of counterproliferation threat issues.

(U) Additionally, each field office has an assigned WMD Program Coordinator. This person is responsible for all WMD hazards at that field office. More importantly, because the WMD program coordinators are funded from division staffing allocations, they are therefore responsible to Headquarters for their operational tasking, not the Special Agents in Charge (SAC) of the field offices. WMDD also has designated division-level "touch points" at Headquarters to assist both the program coordinators and the field offices.[210] WMDD touch points conduct quarterly meetings to ensure information is being shared in a timely and effective way.[211] The touch points also augment the program coordinators' collective understanding of current issues and provide them with subject matter experts who can lend additional assistance managing the WMD portfolio in the field.[212]

(U) Finally, while the TRP process works in tandem with the division-level strategic plans to prioritize threats, much of the effort also takes place at the field-level. The Review Commission, therefore, examined how the FBI, through its field offices and the legal attachés (LEGATs)

---

206 (U) Ibid.
207 (U) Ibid.
208 (U) Ibid., and Memorandum for Record, October 1, 2014.
209 (U) Ibid.
210 (U) Ibid.
211 (U) Ibid.
212 (U) Ibid.

assigned to various US embassies, account for emerging threats both in the United States and overseas.

(U) Field Office Strategic Plans (FOSP)

(U) The FOSPs define how a particular field office addresses threats within its specific area of operations. To do this, FOSPs establish objectives and measures of effectiveness against previously identified threats. Field offices complete their strategic plans after the TRP process produces the master threat list and CSG. Operational divisions subsequently validate these plans. This results in a performance agreement between the SAC, the operational divisions, and the FBI Deputy Director. The FOSPs, in this context, also provide a series of metrics that FBI Headquarters uses to evaluate the SACs' performance. This compels the field offices to prioritize resources according to the details contained within their FOSPs.

(U) Not unexpectedly, the Review Commission found that the TRP and associated FOSPs drive SACs to align resources against identified rather than emerging threats. A field office can reallocate resources. But, potentially, if a field office switched priorities mid-year to address an emerging issue–for example, the 2014 crisis in Ukraine–that field office could come up short on the previously established FOSP metrics during its end of year performance review.[213] To alleviate this concern, the FY14 TRP gave field offices the ability to write a mitigation statement when an emerging threat or critical event adversely affected field office performance against established FOSP metrics. In addition to mitigation statements, field office personnel can document the shifting of resources or changing of priorities anytime in the Integrated Program Management (IPM) Notes Dashboard. This enhancement was initiated in March 2014 for both field office and Headquarters program managers. The Review Commission regards this modification as a positive development in that it minimizes any potential negative ramifications. The next step, from our perspective, would be to reward field offices for the innovative thought, and quite frankly the risks they assume when allocating resources towards emerging threats.[214]

(U) Central Strategic Coordinating Components (CSCC)

(U) CSCCs are responsible for the FBI's domain awareness and analysis. Each field office is required to establish a CSCC. The groups are comprised of small groups of intelligence analysts who are tasked to produce foundational documents such as Domain Intelligence Notes (DINs) and Threat Mitigation Strategies (TMSs). They also expose information gaps and guide special agents' planned or incidental collection efforts. Effective CSCCs are critical to ensuring that field office efforts are threat-based and intelligence-driven.

(U) But during its field office visits, the Review Commission observed an uneven application of the CSCC concept and that many field offices struggled with effectively operating its CSCC. In

---

213 (U) Memorandum for the Record, September 2, 2014. Overall Classification (S//NF); Memorandum for the Record, September 19, 2014.

214 (U) The FBI is aware of the metrics issue and is working to create qualitative metrics in IPM that account for changing threats. The Review Commission understands this is an ongoing process. Memorandum for the Record, November 7, 2014.

the majority of the field offices the Review Commission visited, the CSCCs were not performing their intended functions.[215] Many of the intelligence analysts who were initially assigned to the CSCC had been moved to operational squads to provide tactical support to case agents, leaving the CSCC understaffed and unable to fulfill its primary mission.[216] In some field offices, CSCC analysts were so involved in tactical support that their DINs and TMSs languished until the SAC accounted for them in the office's mid and year-end reviews.[217]

(U) A centerpiece of the FBI's intelligence framework is domain analysis, which entails the ability to understand what is happening in a given area of operations using all available sources of data. Accordingly, domain management is the FBI's systematic process to develop strategic awareness in order to: identify and prioritize threats, vulnerabilities, and intelligence gaps; contribute to the efficient allocation of resources and operational decisions; discover new opportunities for collection; and set tripwires to provide advance warning.[218] The Review Commission strongly believes that the field offices must prioritize collection opportunities to identify, develop, and pursue new intelligence leads in concert with their ongoing investigations.

(U) In many field offices we visited there was only one intelligence analyst left on the CSCC to conduct domain analysis for the field office and even then they spent much of their time mapping existing incidents and/or efforts. There was no observable forward looking aspect to the work. From the Review Commission's observations, even when the DINs and TMSs are produced they are not generally valued at the field office-level as parts of a comprehensive intelligence collection plan (e.g., the plan that establishes the field's baseline knowledge, identifies intelligence gaps, and informs the field's strategy to mitigate new threats).[219] In one field office we were told that an analyst had produced a comprehensive collection plan but it was ignored by the special agents who would have to implement it.[220] We attribute this to a special agent-driven culture that still does not necessarily understand the value of filling intelligence collection requirements and, therefore, renders this overall mission a lower priority than it should be. It can also be attributed to the lack of sufficient leadership to hold field office personnel accountable for intelligence as well as criminal responsibilities

---

215 (U) Some offices demonstrated a much higher comprehension of the CSCC concept and value and consequently provided higher levels of resources to facilitate mission success. The Review Commission would like to commend, however, the one field office that acknowledged that it was struggling with creating an effective CSCC and planned to visit another field office that is believed to be doing a better job so as to learn how others are operating a CSCC and perhaps identify best practices to bring back and implement. Memorandum for the Record, July 28, 2014.

216 (U) One intelligence analyst speculated the CSCC concept was widely misunderstood across the FBI because the benefit to special agents is unclear. The intelligence analyst also estimated that approximately 20 percent of analysts understood the meaning and purpose of the CSCC. Memorandum for the Record, September 17, 2014.

217 (U) Memorandum for the Record, August 14, 2014.

218 (U) Federal Bureau of Intelligence, Directorate of Intelligence, *Intelligence Program Corporate Policy Directive and Policy Implementation Guide*, May 2, 2013: 62.

219 (U) Memorandum for the Record, September 19, 2014.

220 (U) Memorandum for the Record, July 29, 2014.

64

(U) Human Intelligence (HUMINT) Squads

(U) The FBI has made significant progress since September 11, 2011, on the general issue of human intelligence. It is integrated into the National HUMINT Requirements Tasking Center's process, has its own National HUMINT Collection Directives, and has developed a process for requirements development, validation, and collection management.[221] The FBI also increasingly has undertaken joint collection operations with other members of the USIC to mutual advantage.

(U) Despite this progress, however, the Review Commission believes that more attention needs to be paid to the development and use of the HUMINT Squads. There is considerable frustration in the field offices over human intelligence. This appears to stem from either a lack of consistent guidance and methodology from FBI Headquarters,[222] confusion regarding the appropriate division of effort on HUMINT collection between the newly-formed HUMINT squads and traditional operational squads, or the use of metrics that discourage development of sources for anything other than the top banded threats in the TRP.[223] For example, each of the field offices that the Review Commission visited had its own approach to HUMINT collection. Some had detailed all HUMINT personnel to operational squads, while others had created separate HUMINT squads. Then there were those field offices that combined both approaches.[224] Some operational squads valued the support they received from the HUMINT squads, while others questioned these squads' existence, given the FBI's long history of special agents themselves handling human sources. The Review Commission firmly believes that the HUMINT squads are integral to identifying emerging threats, and, therefore, this area requires the focused attention of FBI leadership to better leverage this capability—attention we understand the IB has already committed to provide.

(U) The Review Commission recommends that the SACs require all squads to participate in identifying collection gaps with their local CSCC and the best way forward to close these gaps whether through integrated HUMINT and operational squads or through completely separate entities.[225] The Review Commission also believes that established metrics in this regard should reward innovative thinking and creative efforts toward identifying new threats. The Review Commission heard numerous examples of where existing metrics discourage sources that are not consistently producing actionable intelligence against a Tier I or Tier II banded threat. Thus a source, although very well placed to identify new threats, may be terminated because he/she did not have any material intelligence for a given time. The Review Commission also heard complaints that field offices were penalized in performance reviews for sources who, although not providing intelligence relevant to field office top banded threats, were providing very valuable intelligence addressing USIC priorities, including information that was frequently included in Presidential Daily Briefs. Some HUMINT squads worked to ensure that the FBI was maximizing the value of its sources by identifying issues that existing sources could provide

---

221 (U) Federal Bureau of Investigation, *Confidential Human Source Policy Implementation Guide*, 0499PG, March 9, 2012.
222 (U) Memorandum for the Record, August 12, 2014.
223 (U) Memorandum for the Record, July 28, 2014.
224 (U) Ibid.
225 (U) Memorandum for the Record, September 19, 2014.

beyond the particular case for which the source was recruited.[226] Such best practices should be encouraged. Furthermore, working with joint sources should be credited to both units within a field office, e.g., the HUMINT and operational squads. Prior to FY14, this gap was identified and addressed by the IPM team according to information provided by the FBI following our field office visits. All confidential human source (CHS)-related measures in the FOSPs were amended to sharpen the focus of reporting on lower banded or emerging threats.

(U) Intelligence Dissemination

(U) The Review Commission's visits to the field validated our concerns regarding the HUMINT program, in particular that the metrics being applied to HUMINT were not well-suited to the important role that it needs to play in domain awareness and threat identification. The Review Commission also learned that the reporting process lagged behind the real-time information need requirements of the USIC. The Review Commission learned that routine Intelligence Information Reports (IIR) can take over a month to release and that the Bureau's average release time for an immediate IIR is too slow.[227] More troubling, we were repeatedly told that special agents would prevent the issuing of IIRs on their cases if they felt it would preempt their case.[228] This issue was also raised by multiple senior USIC officials, who believed that not all reportable information was actually being disseminated by the FBI.[229] The timely reporting of information that is potentially useful to law enforcement and USIC partners is an obligation of all members of the USIC. The Review Commission is deeply concerned that timely reporting continues to lag substantially behind USIC norms.

(U) In sum, a truly threat-based and intelligence-driven organization depends on collaborative teams of special agents and intelligence analysts working together effectively. Domain management requires an analytic workforce that elevates intelligence concerns and releases IIRs over case-based objections when necessary to protect national security. Equally importantly, intelligence analysts should be empowered or granted authority to release information to the broader USIC in IIRs using appropriate minimization procedures. If not, then a clearly identified process of appeal must be established in the event that potentially important intelligence is considered unreportable.

---

226 (U) Memorandum for the Record, July 29, 2014.; Memorandum for the Record, September 17, 2014.

227 (U) Memorandum for the Record, September 17, 2014.; Request for Information Response, November 12, 2014. It is important to note these statistics reflect only the time it takes to produce the actual IIR report from an agent's notes. For example, a special agent is still responsible to write up collection in an FD-302 or -1023 before this clock starts. Potentially this means IIR information for priority and immediate reports can languish in the system before the "clock" actually starts on production. IIR production was the most consistent problem cited in the Review Commission's meetings, either in terms of the time the process took or the number of analysts devoted solely to producing IIRs. See, e.g., Memorandum for the Record, August 14, 2014.; Memorandum for the Record, July 28, 2014.; Memorandum for the Record, July 29, 2014.; Memorandum for the Record, July 16, 2014.; Memorandum for the Record, September 17, 2014.; Memorandum for the Record, September 2, 2014.; Memorandum for the Record, August 14, 2014.; Memorandum for the Record, August 15, 2014.; Memorandum for the Record, November 7, 2014.

228 (U) Memorandum for the Record, October 31, 2014.; Memorandum for the Record, November 14, 2014.; Memorandum for the Record, May 21, 2014.

229 (U) Memorandum for the Record, October 31, 2014.; Memorandum for the Record, November 14, 2014.; Memorandum for the Record, November 17, 2014.

(U) Legal Attachés (LEGATs)

(U) The Review Commission concluded that the LEGAT Program has become central to the FBI's mission to protect the United States from terrorist attacks and against foreign intelligence operations and espionage. It is also playing an increasingly critical role in the FBI's cyber mission with over a dozen designated cyber Assistant Legal Attaches (ALATs).[230]

(U) The Review Commission, however, has some concerns about the LEGAT program in its current form. These concerns center on the fact that LEGATs are not yet fully integrated players in country teams with respect to their critical intelligence function. This absence appears to stem at least in part from a lack of analytic resources as well as a focused collection plan. A small minority of LEGATs, for instance, have fulltime intelligence analysts assigned to their post. The Review Commission is encouraged that the International Operations Division (IOD) recognizes the need for increased analytic resources as part of the LEGAT Program. We also recognize and support that this will require increases in financial and personnel resources. The Review Commission does not necessarily recommend that every LEGAT have an accompanying intelligence analyst. Being afforded the opportunity to have an intelligence analyst temporarily assigned to a LEGAT's office, however, represents a potential solution to this problem.[231]

(U) Additionally, the Review Commission found that the LEGAT program currently lacks a uniform approach to ensure those serving as a LEGAT or ALAT are appropriately rewarded in their career progression.[232] We are encouraged that IOD has acknowledged the problem and is working on an appropriate solution. The Review Commission recommends that LEGAT assignments be regarded as a career incentive for the advancement of intelligence analysts as well.

(U) Emerging Threats and a National Security Organization

(U) Having established that FBI strategic plans and prioritization processes do not consistently address emerging threats, and that FBI's HUMINT squads and strategic analysis programs likewise are not postured to identify over-the-horizon threats, the question remains, "what else can the FBI do?" Beyond its recommendations to modify internal FBI plans and processes, as summarized at the end of this chapter, the Review Commission also believes that the FBI should hedge against controversial assumptions and differing views among the wider USIC. Hedging strategies are especially important in a resource-constrained environment and on threats, such as homegrown extremism, for which the FBI holds primary responsibility.

---

230 (U) The Review Commission is especially grateful to personnel from the International Operations Division (IOD), including Lori Welch, Joyce McClelland, Belinda Robinson, and Darleen Malkames, for the invaluable assistance they provided at Headquarters and in support of the Review Commission's visits to foreign LEGAT posts.
231 (U) Memorandum for the Record, October 13, 2014.. For example, one LEGAT office that the Review Commission visited had effectively used an intelligence analyst on a four-week temporary detail to develop a domain analysis and collection plan to help drive the LEGAT's priorities.
232 (U) For some posts this does not appear to be an impediment.

(U) To underscore the importance of this approach, the Review Commission examined emerging counterterrorism threats prioritized by the wider USIC and explored differing assumptions among the USIC, especially as they relate to the US Homeland. The major intelligence agencies, including the FBI, must assess the relative threat of various groups such as state and non-state sponsored violent extremist organizations (VEOs) and homegrown violent extremists (HVEs) to regional and US national security. But each agency should always be acutely aware of how views may differ or change across the agencies. The views, in fact, do differ and change over time as the DNI's National Intelligence Estimate process has demonstrated over the years.

(U) The challenge to individual and collective threat assessment is growing exponentially as the threats to America become more complicated and more globally dispersed. Threats from homegrown violent extremists (HVE), from violent extremist organizations (VEOs), and from US adversaries, state and non-state actors acting alone or together, increasingly threaten denial of service attacks or full assaults against US critical infrastructure.

(U) The Review Commission believes that the FBI must have a robust capability to develop its own threat assessments, but they must reflect awareness of where views differ among and within agencies. FBI assessments need to pay more attention to emerging threats. The Bureau's threat assessments should drive a more dynamic and flexible TRP process. Strategic assessments should inform both division level strategic planning and a corporate strategy to allocate resources for a global intelligence driven investigative service.

(U) Conclusion

(U) The Review Commission concludes that the FBI Counterterrorism Division, Weapons of Mass Destruction Division, Cyber Division, and Intelligence Branch have made progress in their efforts to protect the US Homeland since September 2001. But a number of concerns remain. The Review Commission is troubled that most of the operational divisions reviewed do not consistently use their strategic plans for prioritizing threats and allocating resources. These plans appear to be management strategies more than strategic planning documents. Figure 1. below, Commission Assessment of the FBI's Strategic Plans, illustrates the Review Commission's judgments.

(U) Figure 1: Commission Assessment of the FBI's Strategic Plans

	Threats Driven	Consistent with TRP	Allocates Resources	Management Strategy
Counterterrorism Division Strategic Plan	●	●	●	●
Cyber Division Strategic Plan	○	○	●	●
Weapons of Mass Destruction Division Strategic Plan	●	●	●	●
Directorate of Intelligence Strategic Plan	●	●	●	●

Key ● =satisfactory ○ =in progress ● =unsatisfactory

(U) Similarly, the Review Commission found limited cross-pollination between the operational divisions' plans, which appears to have constrained the ability of the FBI to fully understand the cost of prioritizing tradeoffs between operational divisions at a time of constrained resources. Such a strategy should account for both current and emerging threats. That is, it should be threat-driven by nature. This would also allow for prioritization of resources over a multi-year period. And, it would inform not only division-level strategies but also field office strategies. The Review Commission also found that the operational divisions continue to struggle with visibility on the execution of national priorities at the field office level. CYD and WMDD have attempted to fill these integration gaps through the adaptation of the Cyber threat team, the TExAS Tool, and the WMDD's Coordinators' touch points, which all help facilitate greater field office and Headquarters collaboration of future threats. These approaches represent potential "best practices" for the other divisions.

(U) The FBI, however, should increase its effort to identify and mitigate emerging threats. At the field office level, current structures and metrics inherent in the TRP, CSG, and the strategic plans did not sufficiently encourage or reward the identification of new and emerging threats. To begin to address this issue, starting in FY13, field offices were required to write "Impact Statements" for each operational program to address accomplishments or work on threats that were not systematically captured in the FOSP. The impact statements were also intended to be used to justify shifting resources to work new and emerging threats as opposed to previously identified threats. In some field offices, the basic structure of the CSCC or the HUMINT squads

69

discourages the identification of, and collection against emerging threats. At the Headquarters level, the FBI does not adequately address the underlying assumptions behind its judgments, or those by the wider USIC.[233] The Review Commission recommends that FBI Strategic Plans give greater weight to controversial assumptions and differing views within the wider USIC.

(U) Finally, the Intelligence Branch, whose analysts in many ways underpin the TRP, CSG, and strategic plans, still has work to do on the professionalization of its workforce. We urge the FBI, as part of its new Intelligence Analyst Developmental Plan, to allocate additional resources towards sabbaticals and academic training, detail assignments to other agencies, temporary overseas duty tours, and outreach to scholars on core national security issues. The Review Commission also strongly believes that the FBI can signal the importance and value that it ascribes to its intelligence role by placing intelligence professionals in senior leadership positions within the IB organization.

(U) Recommendations

(U) Over the next several years the FBI faces an evolving threat environment and likely an ongoing constrained fiscal environment. These dual challenges set the context for the recommendations presented below. They underscore the need for the FBI to identify both current and emerging threats, as well as thoroughly understand the assumptions underlying USIC judgments, even if this introduces an inevitable degree of uncertainty. These dual challenges require the FBI's strategic plans to prioritize threats and allocate resources accordingly. They also necessitate that the FBI hedge against uncertainty.

(U) Finding 1: While the FBI has established enterprise-wide strategic focus areas and a strategy map, it does not have an integrated strategic vision to address current and new threats—and an implementable, metric-based plan—that unites its national and global missions, as well as its intelligence and law enforcement, prevention and investigative mandates. Moreover, the relationship between planning and resource allocation is opaque.

(U) Recommendation 1: The Review Commission recommends that the FBI produce a multi-year strategic vision. The plan should integrate division-level strategic plans, drive allocation of resources, direct support functions, and should track with a dynamic, multi-year, threat assessment. The Review Commission also recommends a separate team be established in the Director's office to implement this strategic vision.

- (U) The FBI's strategic vision should integrate all FBI programs; accompanying division and field office plans should be transparent when they differ from the wider USIC and account for different judgments in their mitigation strategies.

- (U) A Congressionally-approved five-year resource plan should accompany the strategic vision in order to execute the FBI's mission in accordance with that vision. Division and field office plans also should drive resource allocations over a five-year period.

---

233 (U) The one exception appears to be the Cyber Division's TExAS Tool. This tool has yet to be fully integrated, but it appears to be transparent in its assumptions and process.

- (U) The FBI should also determine how the FBI's unique capabilities can address DNI and USIC priorities. The FBI, as the domestic DNI representative, should use these priorities to inform the overall strategic vision as well as division and field office strategic plans.

(U) Finding 2: The Review Commission has concerns as to whether or not the Intelligence Branch's Strategic Plan and Program of Analysis will deliver enhanced subject matter expertise in a meaningful timeframe to address emerging threats.

(U) Recommendation 2: The Review Commission recommends that the Intelligence Branch accelerate its implementation of changes to professionalize its workforce of intelligence analysts and staff operations specialists.

- (U) The IB organization should expedite its staffing with intelligence professionals; the IB should leverage the wider USIC much more to help develop a tailored version of strategic analysis.

- (U) The IB should enforce the original intent of the CSCC program to build domain analytic capability at the field offices. This would include tradecraft development, improved access to information, increased analytic collaboration between Headquarters and the field, and enhanced training. Inspections and other evaluations should monitor progress.

- (U) Special Agents in Charge of the field offices should require that HUMINT and operational squads collectively identify collection gaps and mitigation strategies and hold squads accountable for execution. Established metrics and evaluations should reward innovative thinking and efforts to identify new threats.

- (U) The SOS career field should be given clear and consistent managerial guidance, as well as a codified career path that allows for transition into other FBI professional roles.

(U) Finding 3: The Review Commission believes that the LEGAT program plays an important role in global domain awareness and protecting the US Homeland, but it has some concerns about whether or not the program has appropriate levels of support.

(U) Recommendation 3: The Review Commission recommends that the International Operations Division implement changes to demonstrate the value of the LEGAT program.

- (U) IOD should increase intelligence support to the LEGATs. While the Review Commission does not recommend that every LEGAT have an accompanying intelligence analyst overseas, enhanced support could be achieved through designated "touch points" or temporary assignments.

- (U) LEGAT assignments should be rewarded with career incentives for both special agents and intelligence analysts.

(U) Finding 4: The Review Commission believes that the FBI's Threat Review and Prioritization Process successfully holds field offices accountable for addressing current threats, but it does not sufficiently encourage an integrated view of threats or addressing new and emerging threats.

(U) Recommendation 4: The Threat Review and Prioritization Process should be modified to make it more flexible and adaptable to emerging threats to it allow the divisions to augment the TRP as needed. Cross-pollination should take place in accordance within the strategic vision and strategic plans.

- (U) The TRP process should incorporate judgments from long-term USIC forecasts. To the extent that the FBI disagrees with these forecasts, it should be readily transparent in the TRP.

- (U) FBI Headquarters should incorporate two new elements into the TRP metrics: (a) identification of cross-programmatic threats and (b) identification of potential threats.

- (U) The FBI would benefit from instituting systematic quality assurance reviews that incorporate other USIC representation or via external reviewers.

CHAPTER IV
(U) COLLABORATION AND INFORMATION SHARING

(U) Two fundamental tenets are at the heart of the Intelligence Reform and Terrorism Prevention Act of 2004 (IRTPA): 1) that state and local authorities and the American public are now important partners in maintaining the necessary vigilance, and 2) the FBI and the United States Intelligence Community (USIC) need to work in close partnership to prevent terrorist acts against the Homeland. Together, these beliefs have transformed the environment in which the FBI operates and have changed how success in that environment is defined. This section of the report will examine how well the FBI is collaborating and sharing information with partners in this new environment to counter threats to the Homeland.

(U) Key Points

- (U) The FBI has made significant progress in information sharing and collaboration, particularly given the challenges of doing so across such a large, decentralized, and globally dispersed organization.

- (U) The FBI has developed a constructive partnership with the Department of Homeland Security (DHS). FBI's relationships with key USIC partners such as the Central Intelligence Agency (CIA), the National Counterterrorism Center (NCTC), the National Security Agency (NSA), and the Defense Intelligence Agency (DIA) are excellent and still improving.

- (U) The FBI has become a key player on the Office of the Director of National Intelligence (ODNI) staff, and is integrating more into the USIC, although the separation of its budget from the majority of the Department of Defense (DOD) National Intelligence Program continues to be a limiting factor.

- (U) The FBI needs to strengthen its collaboration and information sharing with state and local authorities and the private sector, ensuring the right agencies are represented in Joint Terrorism Task Force (JTTF).

(U) Overall, the Review Commission believes the FBI has made steady progress in collaboration and information sharing, and that is a decidedly good news story in this report (see Figure 1 for a comparison of selected relationships). We looked at the FBI's relationships with what we consider to be some of its most important partners in its national security mission: Department of Justice (DOJ); JTTF partners; DHS; state and local law enforcement; the Department of State; CIA; NCTC; DOD; NSA; and the Directorate of National Intelligence (DNI). We also looked at its relationships with non-federal partners. Certainly, as is the case with other federal agencies, the FBI's relationships across government and the private sector are in various states of evolution depending on the partner, but the trendlines are generally positive. The FBI has done a good job in investing in these relationships, and has detailed or assigned its special agents, intelligence analysts, and other professional staff to a wide array of federal agencies while at the same time hosting these agencies' personnel at the FBI. The Review Commission applauds these efforts and encourages continued investment in these relationships.

(U) Figure 1: Assessment of FBI Information Sharing Relationships

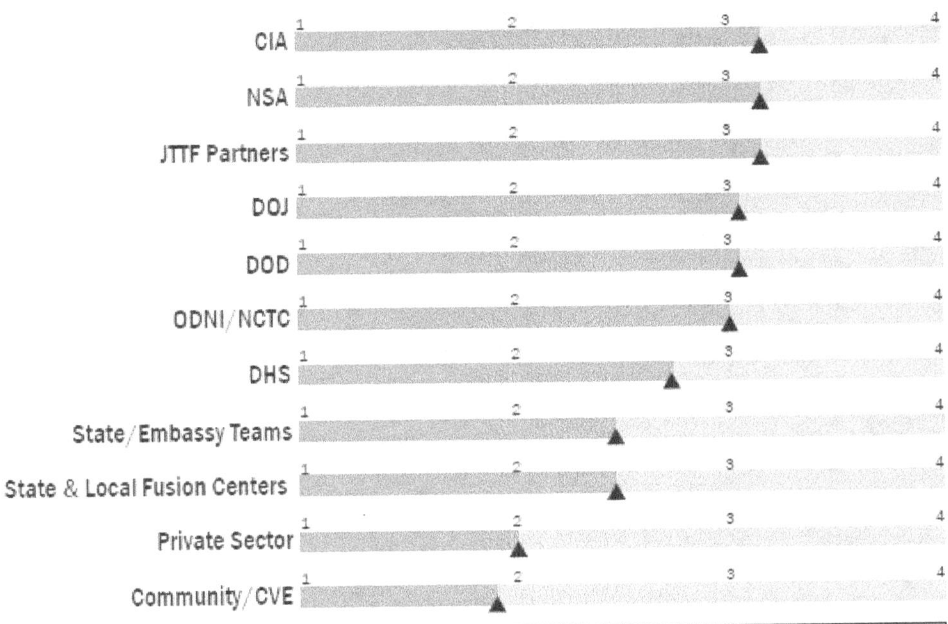

Key
4=Mature, resilient relationship with institutionalized processes and organizational "touchpoints".
3=Solid foundation but processes still evolving; some issues remain to be resolved.
2=Based on transitory shared operational interests and personalities; good but potentially fragile.
1=Not mature. Unclear lanes and authorities preclude optimum effort.

(U) This chart reflects the collective judgments of the Review Commission regarding the relative maturity of these relationships. The data used are subjective and anecdotal, gathered during our interviews of senior leaders in the FBI and other federal agencies, as well as state and local authorities.

(U) According to data maintained by the FBI's Human Resources Division (HRD), the number of FBI employees detailed or assigned to USIC and other US Government agencies, including law enforcement, rose steadily from FY11 to FY13, but dropped off in FY14.[234] During the same period, the number of officers from other federal agencies serving in the FBI was relatively steady, with a notable decline in FY14 (See Figure 2).[235] According to the FBI, the reason for the decline in FY14 is primarily due to the Principal Deputy Director of National Intelligence's (PDDNI) policy that FBI, CIA, DIA, NSA, National Geospatial Agency (NGA), and National Reconnaissance Office (NRO) can no longer post vacancies for non-reimbursable detail assignments on the ODNI joint duty website. This decline was further aggravated by the effects of sequestration.

---

234 (U) FBI/HRD/Law Enforcement and Intelligence Liaison Office (LEICLO) data on detailees and assignees, 2011-2014. See Response to Request for Information, October 16, 2014.
235 (U) How the detailed and assigned employees are arrayed across the Federal Government is explained in more detail later in this chapter.

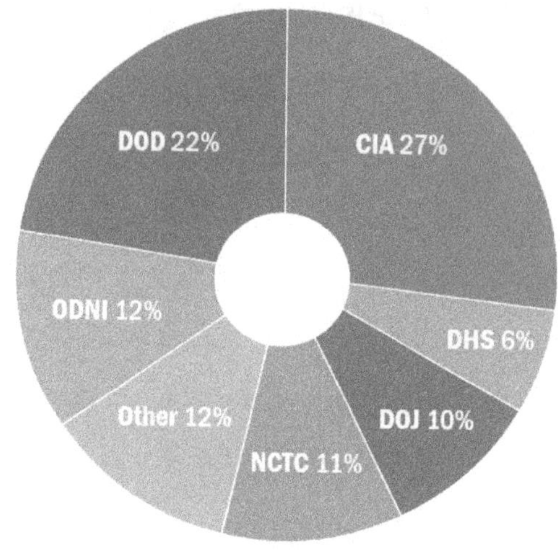

(U) Figure 2: Personnel from FBI detailed to other agencies
(as of Sept. 2014)

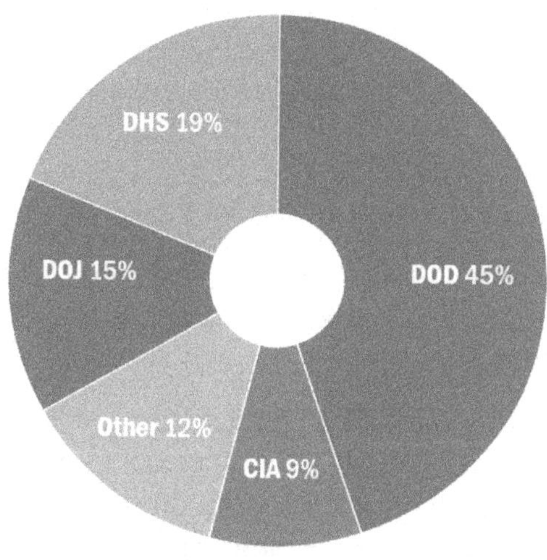

(U) Personnel from other agencies detailed to the FBI
(as of Sept. 2014)

(U) The FBI-DOJ Relationship

(U) The DOJ's National Security Division (NSD) has primary responsibility for oversight of and coordination with the FBI regarding national security and foreign intelligence matters. The relationship between the FBI and DOJ related to national security matters has continued to evolve since the NSD's formation in 2006. The NSD, led by the Assistant Attorney General for National Security, consists primarily of two trial units (the Counterterrorism and Counterespionage Sections) that work with FBI field offices and United States Attorney's Offices to investigate and prosecute national security cases, and the Office of Intelligence

75

(formerly the Office of Intelligence Policy and Review) that coordinates with the FBI's National Security Law Branch (NSLB) on functions related to the Foreign Intelligence Surveillance Act (FISA).

(U) The FBI-DOJ relationship is governed primarily by the Attorney General's Guidelines for Domestic FBI Operations (the "AG Guidelines"), effective December 1, 2008, which authorize the FBI to investigate threats to the national security and collect foreign intelligence.[236] The AG Guidelines describe the NSD's oversight functions, which include regular reviews of FBI national security and foreign intelligence activities at the Headquarters and field office levels. In addition, the AG Guidelines established FBI notification and approval requirements relating to national security matters and requires the FBI to share national security-related information with the White House, other DOJ components, and partner agencies as fully and consistently as possible. Departures from the AG Guidelines must be approved by the FBI Director, the FBI Deputy Director, or by an Executive Assistant Director designated by the Director. The FBI must also provide written notice of such departures to the NSD that will in turn notify the Attorney General and Deputy Attorney General.

(U) The AG Guidelines require the FBI to notify the NSD upon initiation of certain types of investigations concerning threats to national security. The NSD must be provided access to all information obtained by the FBI through activities relating to threats to the national security or foreign intelligence, and the FBI must comply with any requests for reports and information concerning these activities made by the Assistant Attorney General for National Security. In addition, the FBI must provide annual reports to the NSD concerning its foreign intelligence collection program, including information concerning the scope or nature of foreign intelligence collection activities in each field office.

(U) The NSD must also be consulted and, in some instances, approve certain FBI investigative activities for matters involving national security or foreign intelligence. For national security cases, certain communications monitoring activities, as well as otherwise illegal activity to be conducted by an FBI special agent or employee, must be approved by the NSD. The NSD must also be included in the review and approval process for FBI undercover operations involving a threat to the national security.

(U) With respect to the FBI's coordination with DOJ on FISA matters, the passage of the USA PATRIOT Act in 2001 eliminated a perceived legal wall consisting of court rules and internal DOJ procedures surrounding the use of FISA warrants that barred FBI intelligence agents from collaborating with criminal investigators and prosecutors. Following enactment of the USA PATRIOT Act, FBI special agents working on intelligence cases were authorized to disseminate to criminal prosecutors and investigators all relevant foreign intelligence information, including information obtained pursuant to FISA, in accordance with applicable minimization standards and other statutory requirements. Correspondingly, the procedures authorized prosecutors and

---

236 (U) The current AG Guidelines superseded several older authorities, including the *Attorney General's Guidelines on General Crimes, Racketeering Enterprise and Terrorism Enterprise Investigations,* May 30, 2002, among others.

criminal special agents to advise FBI agents working intelligence cases on the use of FISA information.

(U) Feedback from special agents and supervisors on the FBI-DOJ relationship focused primarily on the NSD's perceived inability to quickly approve FBI requests to conduct investigative activities in national security matters. Special agents complained that the NSD was too slow in reviewing FISA applications and submitting them to the Foreign Intelligence Surveillance Court (FISC) for approval.[237] Though perceived delays could sometimes be attributable to the FBI, the general perception was that the NSD works too slowly and has been insufficiently aggressive in supporting the FBI's surveillance requests.[238]

(U) The Review Commission identified concerns in some field offices-about the narrowness of the FISA statute's lone wolf provision, which only applies to non-U.S. persons.[239] Several field offices noted that this left the FISA bar particularly high with respect to surveillance applications involving homegrown violent extremists (HVEs) with no identified connection to a foreign power.[240]

(U) The Review Commission received mixed feedback on the relationship between various FBI field offices and their respective United States Attorney's Offices. Special agents and supervisors at several field offices complained that United States Attorney's Offices often seemed unwilling to bring criminal prosecutions in national security-related cases, particularly those involving classified materials.[241] In one instance, special agents indicated they had greater success working with state and local prosecutors who were more willing to prosecute certain cases (such as bomb and identity hoax charges) than their federal counterparts.[242] However, other field offices praised the support they received from their United States Attorney's Office in the national security context, particularly those willing to bring prosecutions in support of FBI extraterritorial squads.[243]

(U) Joint Terrorism Task Force Partners

(U) The most important entity for addressing the terrorist threat in the Homeland is arguably the JTTF. The first JTTF was established in New York City in 1980. Today there are over 100 JTTFs—including nearly 70 established after 9/11—and they comprise the core of domestic counterterrorism efforts in America today.[244] JTTFs are well-suited to fighting terrorism in a post-9/11 world, providing the mechanism for collaboration with partners from a wide variety of

---

237 (U) Memorandum for the Record, June 13, 2014.
238 (U) Memorandum for the Record, September 2, 2014.
239 (U) This issue did not apply to any of the five cases described in Chapter II, all of which involved US persons.
240 (U) Memorandum for the Record, June 2, 2014; Memorandum for the Record, June 13, 2014.
241 (U) Memorandum for the Record, July 15, 2014.; Memorandum for the Record, August 11, 2014.; Memorandum for the Record, August 14, 2014.
242 (U) Memorandum for the Record, July 17, 2014.
243 (U) Memorandum for the Record, September 17, 2014.
244 (U)   FBI Briefing, *The Joint Terrorism Task Force (JTTF) and the National Joint Trerorism Task Force (NJTTF)*, March 3, 2014.

other federal, state, local, tribal, and territorial law enforcement entities.[245] The Review Commission's field interviews have shown that the JTTFs, though governed by a standard memorandum of understanding among participating agencies, are a flexible organizational concept: every field office staffs and organizes its JTTF differently. We asked Special Agent in Charge (SACs) of several field offices whether or not they felt they had the right personnel in the right positions at their JTTFs and answers varied; one field office characterized the staffing of Task Force Officer (TFO) positions as informal and intermittent.[246] All field office leaders emphasized that TFOs played important roles at their respective JTTFs, and many wished they had more of them. In turn, TFOs generally felt like full members of their JTTF team; however, we discovered that in one field office the TFOs did not have the same access to case information in Guardian and Sentinel as their FBI counterparts.[247] The Review Commission learned that there are a variety of possible reasons for this, including failure to complete required training to access datasets and lack of permissions for legacy datasets that are linked to the system.[248] It is also possible that TFOs seeking specific information on a case or lead simply could not find it because of a programming flaw in Sentinel's search and indexing function.[249]

(U) TFOs are a key avenue for sharing pertinent terrorist information with state and local authorities, and therefore TFOs investigating cases with their FBI counterparts need all pertinent information in order to see cases and leads through to their logical ends. The FBI is committed to providing TFOs equal access to case information and has made repeated attempts to resolve this issue, most recently in the aftermath of the Boston Marathon bombing.[250] At that time, FBI Headquarters issued guidance clarifying that not only should TFOs have equal access to case information, they were also encouraged to look for information in Guardian and Sentinel relevant to their home office and to share it, once appropriately cleared by the Supervisory Special Agent (SSA). The SSAs were directed to routinely approve requests to share such information, even if it required permission from a grand jury or originating control authority. However, the combined Inspectors' General of the USIC report on the Boston Marathon bombing went even further, recommending a more proactive approach that included establishing a procedure for notifying state and local representatives on JTTFs when a counterterrorism assessment of a subject residing in or having a nexus to a TFO's area of responsibility is conducted. This is both

---

245 (U) The FBI's standard memorandum of understanding with any police department states, "[i]n order to ensure that there is a robust capability to deter, defeat and respond vigorously to terrorism in the U.S. or against any U.S. interest, the FBI recognizes the need for all federal, state and local, and tribal agencies that are involved in fighting terrorism to coordinate and share information and resources." FBI, *Standard Memorandum of Understanding Between the Federal Bureau of Investigation and (any particular agency)*, Template version May 10, 2013.

246 (U) Memorandum for the Record, June 13, 2014.

247 (U) Memorandum for the Record, July 29, 2014.; Memorandum for the Record, August 4, 2014.. When the issue was brought to the field office's attention it worked promptly to identify the cause of the problem and remedied it.

248 (U) Memorandum for the Record, July 28, 2014.; Memorandum for the Record, August 4, 2014.

249 (U) Interviews with Sentinel users and responses to a detailed survey revealed dissatisfaction with the system's search and indexing functions. Regarding the search function, only 42 percent of respondents replied they received the results they needed. This issue is currently being addressed by the Bureau. See US Department of Justice Office of Inspector General, *"Audit of the Status of the Federal Bureau of Investigation's Sentinel Program"* Audit Report 14-31September 2014: 6 and Appendix IV.

250 (U) See content of e-mail from Deputy Director Sean Joyce to all SACs July 22, 2013 (attached to letter from Sean Joyce to Charles Ramsey, November 26, 2013; Memorandum for the Record, August 4, 2014.

to ensure notification of state and local authorities, but also to ensure that they have the opportunity to share relevant information with the FBI.[251] In its report on the Boston Marathon bombings the House Homeland Security Committee made a similar recommendation, calling for a modification to the Memorandum of Understanding (MOU) between the FBI and other agencies that prevents the sharing of information outside the JTTFs without FBI approval.[252]

(U) The Review Commission believes the FBI needs to address the data access issues in a way that provides systemic safeguards, such as alerts to TFOs and their supervisors when their accesses have expired, or some positive way to ensure that they and the JTTF leadership have equal situational awareness. We believe the FBI is doing this, and encourage them to accelerate that process. However, the Review Commission believes that the changes promulgated to the field offices and the modifications to the JTTF memorandum in the wake of the Boston Marathon bombing, while improvements, do not go far enough to qualify as a policy of proactive notification to state and local authorities.[253] Because there is no way to know that the right TFO will be present on the JTTF at the right time, the policy of placing the burden for identifying information to share with local jurisdictions solely on the TFO seems ill-founded. JTTFs conduct regularly scheduled Executive Board meetings and conference calls to share threat information, but for real-time developments, these procedures are obviously not sufficient. While SACs assured us that in developing incidents involving local jurisdictions they would pick up the telephone and call their counterparts, the Review Commission believes that policy guidelines on the responsibilities of the SAC to proactively notify state and local authorities under certain circumstances would be beneficial and in the long term interests of the FBI.

(U) The FBI is enhancing the capabilities of state and local law enforcement officers through two courses at its academy at Quantico: an eight-day JTTF Operations Course, and the National Academy's 10-week residential training program for those at the state and local level who may not be members of the JTTF.[254] The JTTF course was adjusted following the Webster Commission's recommendation that TFOs receive greater training and access to FBI information. While the JTTF training is only made available to JTTF members, the National

---

251 (U) See *IG Summary of Information Handling*, 25.

252 (U) See House Homeland Security Committee Report, *The Road to Boston: Counterterrorism Challenges and Lessons from the Marathon Bombings,* March 2014.

253 (U) The FBI has acknowledged that its standard JTTF MOU is an administrative— not a policy—document. It is intended "to ensure compliance with requirements such as FISA minimization rules, protection of sources and methods, and the need to prevent inappropriate disclosure of information originating and controlled by other intelligence services," according to an FBI memorandum responding in part to a letter from the Major Cities Chiefs Association (MCCA). See Deputy Director Sean Joyce Letter to Charles Ramsey, November 26, 2013.

254 (U) JTTF course design and training objectives: The JTTF Operations Course is sponsored by the CTD's Continuing Education and Professional Development Unit (CEPDU). This eight-day course addresses the congressional mandate that all JTTF personnel receive training to familiarize them with the standard paperwork, policies, procedures, operations, case investigative techniques, and database they will use as JTTF members. After completion of the course, learners will be able to: Describe the roles and responsibilities of the Task Force Officer (TFO) within the FBI, as well as the policies and procedures that govern their actions as FBI detailees; describe the threats posed by domestic and international terrorists based on the case studies and legal briefings provided; and use FBI systems and recourses (including DWS, DIVS, Guardian, Clearwater, and Sentinel/ACS) at a basic level of proficiency sufficient to conduct their duties as TFOs. For National Academy training nominations see: https://www.fbi.gov/about-us/national-academy/na-nominations.

Academy training reaches law enforcement personnel who may have no relationship to the JTTF or Field Intelligence Groups (FIGs), but who may provide critical indicators regarding radicalization or plots based on their observations of the communities they serve. The JTTF training covers FBI operations and databases, policies, procedures, case investigative techniques and standard paperwork, as well as education on threats posed by domestic and international terrorists. The National Academy training program includes classes that address radicalization among youth offenders, how terrorist groups globally integrate to expand their influence, critical incident response to terrorism and homeland security events, understanding contemporary terrorist threats, and training for law enforcement leaders on counterterrorism prevention programs. Both programs include legal training. The JTTF training is offered eight times a year, and requires eleven prerequisite courses be completed through the FBI's Virtual Academy prior to attending the JTTF training. The National Academy training is offered four times a year.

(U) The FBI-DHS Relationship

(U) The FBI's relationship with DHS has improved greatly in the past 18 months, although it is a work in progress. The FBI's relationship with DHS was challenging from the beginning because the broad statutory language establishing the department's responsibilities overlapped significantly with the FBI's mission space. In addition, for many years, DHS struggled to perform many of its responsibilities. The introduction of a new department with a mission to share information with local law enforcement and the private sector, areas where the FBI had developed long-standing relationships in support of its missions, was almost certainly going to result in bureaucratic conflict. However, the relationship has improved, and from a counterterrorism perspective is currently viewed as very constructive by senior leaders at DHS. Conversely, in the cyber realm, the FBI's relationship with the department has not been as good, due to a lack of clarity on division of effort.

(U) The relationship with DHS is really multiple relationships, because the FBI works closely with DHS Headquarters (Office of Intelligence and Analysis (I&A) and Office of Operations Coordination), as well as with many DHS components: the Transportation Security Agency (TSA), Customs and Border Protection (CBP), Immigration and Customs Enforcement (ICE), Homeland Security Investigation (HSI), and the Coast Guard primarily on counterterrorism issues. In addition, the FBI works closely with the National Programs and Protection Directorate (a Headquarters element that is also an operational element), Secret Service, and ICE on cyber issues. The relationship with I&A is centered on intelligence and information sharing with state and local law enforcement, primarily via the fusion centers. Over the years, that relationship has matured and resulted in an improved and standardized process for issuing joint products to the field on homeland threats.[255]

(U) The creation of the Counterterrorism Coordinator position at DHS in 2010 provided a focal point for operational coordination, particularly on topics such as visa overstays, aviation security procedures, outreach to faith-based communities, and department-wide response to emerging

---

255 (U) Memorandum for the Record, October 31, 2014.; Memorandum for the Record, November 11, 2014.; Memorandum for the Record, November 14, 2014.; and Memorandum for the Record, November 25, 2014.

threats.[256] Interaction with DHS Headquarters has been further simplified now that the Undersecretary for Intelligence and Analysis is also the Counterterrorism Coordinator.[257] The joint procedures that have evolved, including shared video-teleconferences with federal and local stakeholders in the field, have been well-received by local partners who want to see Washington speaking with one voice whenever possible.[258]

(U) The direct relationships with DHS components are generally managed in the context of the JTTF. ICE is viewed by many field offices as a particularly valuable member of the JTTF.[259] ICE is committed to the JTTF concept and strives to have at least one TFO in every JTTF. However, in our conversation with a former senior HSI official, he stated his belief that the JTTFs have become more FBI-centric over time, and that the contributions of the TFOs are not valued as they were in the immediate aftermath of 9/11.[260] The Review Commission heard numerous complaints at multiple locations regarding the perceived lack of coordination between HSI and the FBI and other government agencies, including overseas. This has led to a lack of trust and confidence.

(U) The value of CBP travel data was generally recognized, and has repeatedly demonstrated its utility in counterterrorism cases. The process by which this information is shared between the CBP TFO and the FBI within the JTTF was routinized as a result of the Boston Marathon bombing, as discussed in Chapter II. A senior CBP official expressed a similar commitment to the JTTF concept and the goal to have CBP on every one; he also cited the positive relationship between CBP attaches overseas and the FBI legal attachés (LEGATs).[261]

(U) Only one field office registered complaints about DHS in the context of the JTTF. The complaints centered on mission creep and overlap, duplication of effort, and lack of information sharing and prior coordination. Thus, the field office noted instances in which DHS entities crossed into FBI's lanes, conducted parallel targeting initiatives, and did not uniformly share information.[262] Many of the concerns and issues expressed by this field office revealed a lack of understanding of the DHS missions to enforce border and aviation security and prosecute crimes like human trafficking. Most of the concerns reflected a feeling of being blindsided by ICE or CBP actions such as removing individuals from planes or arresting subjects the FBI was watching without prior FBI knowledge. Conversations with former and current ICE and CBP officials indicate that the border area (including international airports), where DHS has significant authorities and responsibilities, presents a unique operating environment for both agencies where greater coordination is necessary to prevent unintended disruption of operations. In general, coordination works well, and the chains of command of all involved agencies are

---

256 (U) See "Statement of John Cohen, before the House Homeland Security Committee, Subcommittee on Border and Maritime Security, "Ten Years after 9/11: Can Terrorists Still Exploit our Visa System?," September 12, 2011, https://www.dhs.gov/news/2011/09/12/statement -john-cohen-principal-deputy-coordinator-counterterrorism-house-homeland.

257 (U) Memorandum for the Record, November 14, 2014.

258 (U) Memorandum for the Record, December 4, 2014.

259 (U) Memorandum for the Record, July 13, 2014.; and Memorandum for the Record, July 29, 2014.

260 (U) Memorandum for the Record, November 5, 2014.

261 (U) Memorandum for the Record, November 14, 2014.

262 (U) Memorandum for the Record, September 18, 2014.

committed to maintaining constructive relationships. FBI special agents' increased familiarity with TSA/CBP's targeting rules for travelers to the United States and how they are devised and implemented, as well as FBI's continued sharing with DHS of information on persons under investigation whom the FBI does not want to undergo secondary screening or be detained, might improve coordination at airports.

(U) While the lanes in the road between DHS and the FBI vis-à-vis local law enforcement still overlap, the two have developed workable procedures for cooperation despite the current ambiguity. Clarity and clear divisions of responsibilities are required. The same progress does not appear in DHS and FBI interactions with the private sector. DHS is charged with critical infrastructure protection and the vast majority of such infrastructure is in private hands.[263] There is significant overlap between DHS and the FBI in working with these critical infrastructure firms, who also tend to be important strategic partners for the FBI, and are often targets of cyber and other criminal activity. A contributing factor to this confusing situation appears to be that there is no single effective locus for private sector responsibility in either agency despite the recent creation of the office of private sector engagement in the FBI.[264]

(U) The challenge for both DHS and the FBI in coordinating cyber relationships is due in large part to the lack of clarity at the national level on cyber roles and responsibilities. While Washington tries to coordinate the overlapping responsibilities of various federal agencies, the private sector is left in the dark.[265] The Review Commission has been impressed by the Cyber Division's approach to the global cyber threat, but notes the FBI is limited in its cyber efforts by the muddled national cyber architecture that will continue to affect the relationship with DHS. This issue was raised with the Review Commission by various senior current and former officials, but is beyond the FBI's ability to address in isolation.[266]

(U) The FBI-State and Local Law Enforcement Relationship

(U) The Office of the Program Manager for the Information Sharing Environment, which had been created pursuant to IRTPA, made fusion centers the nation's focal points for the sharing of terrorist threat information among federal, state, and local law enforcement and first responders. The FBI, however, initially looked upon the fusion centers as potential competitors to its own FIGs or JTTFs. Today there are approximately 77 federally-recognized fusion centers in the United States. These centers vary greatly in their levels of development.[267] The FBI now appears committed to working with these fusion centers and has established a policy framework to do so.

---

263 (U) See Homeland Security Presidential Directive, HSPD-7, *Directive on Critical Infrastructure Identification, Prioritization and Protection,* June 17, 2004, accessed at www.whitehouse.gov/sites/default/files/omb/memoranda/fy04/m-04-15.pdf.
264 (U) See for example discussion of Cyber Divisions, responsibility for InfraGard on p. 102.
265 (U) Memorandum for the Record, November 21, 2014.
266 (U) Memorandum for the Record, November 25, 2014.
267 (U) The Constitution Project, *Recommendations for Fusion Centers: Preserving Privacy & Civil Liberties While* Protecting Against Crime & Terrorism, August 2012, http://www.constitutionproject.org/pdf/fusioncenterreport.pdf.

(U) In August 2011, the FBI established a fusion center engagement plan for field offices to use to gauge their levels of collaboration and interaction with their local fusion centers.[268] In the plan, the FBI identifies liaison, basic, and enhanced levels of engagement, based on the maturity of the fusion center. Liaison-level engagement is typified by limited interaction between Bureau officials and local analysts—with no meaningful joint products or shared missions—but with continuing communication in order to gauge the fusion center's progress. Basic-level engagement reflects shared priorities, occasional joint products, and more sharing of FBI information. With enhanced-level engagement, a fusion center has the infrastructure to host FBI personnel, there is a shared mission focus, and frequent information sharing occurs. Currently, only about one third of the fusion centers are considered truly effective forums for collaboration and cooperation.[269] The FBI has more than 90 personnel assigned to fusion centers in some capacity, with 12 fusion centers collocated with the FBI.[270]

(U) During the Review Commission's field office visits, we observed basic to enhanced levels of interaction. In one field division where basic level engagement occurs, FIG analysts host periodic strategic-level briefings for state decision-makers at the fusion center regarding foreign threats and their implications to the region.[271] In another field division, the FBI only maintains a part-time presence at the state center; local authorities believe that the level of information sharing with the FBI, and concomitantly with the JTTF, suffers as a consequence of this staffing decision.[272] In a third field division, the FBI's fusion center relationship has developed over the past 10 years from a basic, personality-driven relationship to an enhanced one, and the fusion center has assigned members to the local JTTF.[273]

(U) In most cases, the FBI appears to have developed a structured way to gauge the right level of engagement with the fusion centers, although the fusion centers that do not have a permanent FBI presence will continue to express the desire for more FBI interaction. A recurrent issue raised by state and local authorities in our field visits was their perception that sharing with the Bureau is still too much of a one-way street, with the prime example being the lack of feedback on Suspicious Activity Reports (SAR) reporting via Guardian. The FBI is working to improve its relationship with state and local fusion centers in general, and directly with partner law enforcement agencies, by providing feedback on SARs entered by the fusion centers or directly by law enforcement partners into the FBI's Guardian system. Such feedback is now pushed automatically from the classified Guardian system into the unclassified eGuardian portal.

---

268 (U) Federal Bureau of Investigation, *FBI Engagement with Fusion Center* (undated).
269 (U) Memorandum for the Record, May 5, 2014.
270 (U) A senior FBI official has indicated the Bureau is trying to raise this number. Memorandum for the Record, July 22, 2014.
271 (U) Memorandum for the Record, July 30, 2014.
272 (U) Memorandum for the Record, August 14, 2014.
273 (U) Memorandum for the Record, July 15, 2014.

(U) The FBI-Department of State Relationship

(U) For the purposes of this report, we focus on the FBI's engagement with the Department of State in the context of its most important relationship overseas—as key members of the country team in US diplomatic missions around the globe. In interviews the Review Commission conducted with FBI LEGATs and State's Regional Security Officers (RSOs) in multiple US embassies in Europe and Asia, we found that relations between the two are generally constructive, although the FBI-State relationship is one of several relationships among US law enforcement entities overseas (e.g., the Drug Enforcement Administration (DEA), HSI, ICE, CBP, and the Coast Guard). The Review Commission found, however, that several LEGATs expressed frustration with the Department of State, particularly with respect to the lack of support they received regarding space, facilities, and getting the positions they needed in a timely manner.[274] The Review Commission notes that the FBI is not alone among US agencies facing such challenges in overseas diplomatic missions.

(U) Several senior State Department officers offered their perspectives on how to further advance the LEGAT's mission and bona fides during interviews with the Review Commission. Uniformly, these officers noted that LEGAT offices consistently punched above their weight, as they often were the more lightly staffed law enforcement bodies in embassies. Recognizing the critical role for the FBI overseas, the State officers also strongly recommended that the Bureau needed to invest more heavily in their LEGAT offices and to fill positions with special agents at the more senior levels. They also suggested better preparation for FBI officers serving overseas, to include more regional and substantive expertise on the countries they were responsible for, and to more generally invest heavily in the LEGAT program. LEGATs, however, appeared divided on the aspect of language training as part of this preparation. One LEGAT noted that language training before reporting to his foreign post was insufficient, but added that he was not sure that having the local language mattered substantially.[275] In contrast, another LEGAT indicated that knowing the national language helped immensely to boost his credibility with host nation counterparts.[276] The Review Commission believes that language skills and linguist talents are critically important.

(U) The FBI-CIA Relationship

(U) Collaboration and information sharing between the FBI and CIA is probably at its highest level, owing to the urgency for cooperation forged in the aftermath of the 9/11 attacks, growing familiarity with each other's mission and remit, and recent legislation and bilateral agreements that clarify the agencies' respective roles and responsibilities. Overseas LEGATs and COSs have expressed to the Review Commission that coordination and information sharing works extremely well.[277]

---

274 (U) Ibid.

275 (U) Memorandum for the Record, October 9, 2014.

276 (U) Memorandum for the Record, October 10, 2014.

277 (U) See, e.g., Memorandum for the Record, October 14, 2014. ; and Memorandum for the Record, October 14, 2014.; and Memorandum for the Record, October 16, 2014.

(U) The IRTPA, as well as E.O. 13355 signed by President George W. Bush in 2004 that amended E.O. 12333, created new structures to enhance unity of effort, inter-agency cooperation, and information sharing among agencies.[278] The creation of the DNI and the NCTC, in particular, provided additional venues with the potential to improve engagement and information sharing between the FBI and CIA (see section on the relationship between FBI and NCTC below). The 9/11 Commission Report gave former Director Mueller appropriate credit for making significant progress in improving the FBI's intelligence capabilities, while also noting that "advances have been made in improving the Bureau's information technology systems and in increasing connectivity and information sharing with intelligence community agencies."[279]

(U) The relationship between the FBI and CIA domestically and overseas appears to be on solid ground, and is arguably the strongest it has been in their collective history. A key component contributing to the health of the relationship is the Memorandum of Understanding (MOU) Concerning Overseas and Domestic Activities of the Central Intelligence Agency and the Federal Bureau of Investigation signed in 2005 (hereafter referred to as the 2005 MOU), which lays out the respective roles of the CIA (COS) and FBI (LEGAT or SAC) in such activities, with the objective of ensuring the full and seamless coordination and cooperation between the CIA and FBI in both the overseas and domestic arenas. The 2005 MOU provides specificity to the respective responsibilities and authorities of the FBI and CIA laid out in broad terms in E.O. 12333 and E.O. 13355, as well as the subsequent amendment signed by President Bush in 2008 (E.O. 13470). The 2005 MOU assigns clear authorities and lead responsibilities to FBI and CIA based on core missions. Importantly, the 2005 MOU provides clear guidance as to how the FBI and CIA are to coordinate their activities and keep each other informed of those activities or entities that cross bureaucratic boundaries. In addition, the 2005 MOU is explicit regarding the agencies' obligations to share information in certain situations and provides reporting and dissemination guidelines.[280] The FBI and CIA approved a joint message in 2012 that reemphasized and clarified the foundational elements of the 2005 MOU noting that the "joint message is also intended to prevent misunderstandings which occasionally occur by narrow interpretation of responsibilities as well as avoiding duplication of effort which is especially important in the current environment of scarce resources."

(U) In our interviews of CIA Station Chiefs and LEGATs abroad, all emphatically stated that the relationship was collegial with each confident that his or her counterpart was consistently forthcoming with information relevant to the other's remit. Each was well aware of the 2005 MOU, but in no instance did either the COS or LEGAT indicate that they ever found it necessary to cite its language to justify an action. In response to the Review Commission's inquiries, several COSs offered suggestions on how their counterpart LEGAT office could be improved. In sum, they noted that LEGAT offices needed additional visibility and gravitas within the

---

278 (U) IRTPA; Executive Order (E.O.) No. 12,333, 40 Fed. Reg. 235, December 4, 1981 (as amended by E.O. 13234 (2003), 1355 (2004), and 13470 (2008)); and E.O. 13355, 69 Fed. Reg. 53593, September 1, 2004.
279 (U) *9/11 Commission Report,* 425, E.O. 12,333.
280 (U) Memorandum of Understanding (MOU) Concerning Overseas and Domestic Activities of the Central Intelligence Agency and the Federal Bureau of Investigation, 2005.; E.O. 13,470, 73 Fed. Reg. 51209, July 30, 2008.

Embassy, especially with respect to their relationships with other US law enforcement agencies and the State Department's RSO in particular. One COS noted that the LEGAT should be more experienced and senior in the FBI so as to compete on a more competitive level within the embassy, including with the RSO and other law enforcement agencies. Moreover, the same COS suggested that the LEGAT should be given similar authorities as the senior DEA officer in country, allowing the LEGAT to interact on par with SACs in field offices in the US. This COS noted that in his experience LEGATs were sometimes pushed around by SACs stateside in field offices and lacked the authority to control their respective overseas areas of responsibility (AORs). Several COSs noted that CIA knew more about the travel of confidential human sources (CHSs) from their Headquarters or National Resources (NR) stations than did the LEGAT because of this apparent inability or unwillingness of FBI field offices to adequately keep the LEGAT informed of such travel.[281]

(U) Similarly, the 2005 MOU provides a useful framework for the interaction of the SACs in the 56 field offices with the CIA's NR Division Station and Base Chiefs across the United States. Field office visits reinforced that relationships with NR in the domestic field are good.[282] Senior USIC officials with broad experience in human intelligence indicated that the FBI and NR were jointly producing great intelligence, and had developed excellent procedures for proper hand-offs of sources from one entity to the other.[283]

(U) FBI and CIA Detailees and Assignees

(U) The FBI has invested heavily over the past several years in placing its officers in CIA units, which has no doubt improved cooperation and information sharing, as well as familiarity with CIA and its operational tradecraft. The value to the FBI's ability to perform strategic analysis of emerging threats is far less clear. While the Review Commission knows that the FBI has embedded its officers in the CIA since the 1980s, the trend has increased over the years, particularly after 9/11. Recognizing that it needed to centralize management of the deployment of FBI personnel from across the individual divisions, the FBI leaders directed HRD in 2011 to establish a new office to do precisely that.[284] Since then, the FBI has compiled detailed data on its integration with other federal agencies for 2011-2014.[285]

---

281 (U) The Review Commission notes that the FBI is trying to remedy this problem. See p. 104 later in this Chapter for information on the FBI's intention to apply a best practice of CTD's Counterterrorism HUMINT Operational Unit (CHOU) across the Bureau. Memorandum for the Record, October 9, 2014.; Memorandum for the Record, October 14, 2014.; Memorandum for the Record, October 16, 2014.

282 (U) Memorandum for the Record, July 23, 2014.; Memorandum for the Record, August 11, 2014.; Memorandum for the Record, September 2, 2014.

283 (U) The Review Commission regrets that we were not able to ascertain the views of CIA/NR on these issues. The Review Commission submitted requests for briefings from CIA on a broad number of topics, including with NR, via the FBI Deputy Director's office. We do not know why CIA was unable to meet with us. Memorandum for the Record, November 14, 2014. ; and Memorandum for the Record, November 17, 2014.

284 (U) Memorandum for the Record, September 26, 2014.

285 (U) FBI/Human Resources Division/Law Enforcement and Intelligence Community Liaison Office (FBI/HRD/LEICLO) provided data as of September 2014. Response to Request for Information, October 16, 2014.

(U) While a large investment in aggregate, the details of the FBI's deployment to the CIA show a distinct bias towards special agents vice professional staff, such as intelligence analysts and staff operations specialists (SOS). Of FBI employees at CIA as of September 2014, 71 percent were special agents while the remaining were professional staff, of which the majority were intelligence analysts. The data suggest, however, that these intelligence analysts were assigned primarily to CIA units to serve as collection managers in support of operations. In the data provided by HRD, the Review Commission did not identify the forward deployment of FBI intelligence analysts to units in the CIA's Directorate of Intelligence, thus limiting these analysts' exposure to and experience with more strategic, forward-leaning analysis that would further help the FBI in envisioning and articulating the future threat environment it faces.[286]

(U) The FBI-NCTC Relationship

(U) Compared to its long-term relationship with CIA, the FBI's engagement with NCTC is far more recent owing to NCTC's creation in 2004 through the IRTPA, but it is also far less robust from a human resources standpoint. That said, unlike the assignment of its personnel to CIA, the FBI's human resource commitment to NCTC is heavily weighted toward intelligence analysts with a modest investment in counterterrorism operations. While NCTC's Directorate of Intelligence (DI) provides ample opportunities for FBI intelligence analysts to gain invaluable experience working across the USIC and produce a diverse range of intelligence products for national-level consumers, it is less clear whether the full value of this experience is recognized, rewarded, or used to the Bureau's advantage when the analysts return to the FBI. On the operations side, the FBI has limited investment in NCTC's Directorate of Strategic Operational Planning (DSOP).[287]

(U) The main message the Review Commission heard from NCTC regarding the FBI's forward deployed intelligence analysts was the perception of these analysts that they were still considered second-class citizens by special agents retaining a "veto power" over their analytic products.[288] As an example of this dynamic, joint NCTC-FBI analytic products would sail through the coordination process only to be derailed or delayed by special agents who would say that they either disagreed with the analysis or that disseminating the analysis would hurt a case.[289] Analysts believed that special agents' reluctance to have aspects of their cases in products written for senior policymakers—including the FBI Director—were driven by a perception that

---

286 (U) Ibid. CIA's presence in the FBI shows a similar preference for operations versus analysis. As of September 2014, CIA had forward deployed several officers to FBI, with almost all assigned to operational divisions and field offices. A CIA official currently serves as the Associate Executive Assistant Director for the National Security Branch.

287 (U) Memorandum for the Record, October 31, 2014.; FBI/HRD/LEICLO data, Response to Request for Information, October 16, 2014.

288 (U) The Review Commission has noted this characterization of the analyst-agent relationship is a persistent theme that pervades the FBI's organizational culture. A 2005 DOJ audit of the FBI's analytic program concluded that a lack of respect for analysts, or analysts feeling like "second class citizens continues to be a major concern…and needs to be remedied." See U.S. Department of Justice, Office of the Inspector General, *"The Federal Bureau of Investigation's Efforts to Hire, Train, and Retain Intelligence Analysts,"* Audit Report 05-20, May 2005; 111.

289 (U) Memorandum for the Record, October 31, 2014.

these products would be read as report cards on special agents' performance and would likely result in more work for them.[290] It appears to the Review Commission that there is clear dichotomy in the way that special agents perceive and value intelligence analysts' work; at the case or tactical-level their contributions are valued but strategic-level analysis for a broader national security audience is sometimes viewed as being at odds with FBI operational requirements.

(U) The Review Commission has heard selective reports that a significant number of FBI analysts serving in NCTC do not wish to return to the Bureau following their details, as they do not perceive their work is valued by the FBI as much as it is by NCTC and the broader USIC.[291] The Review Commission does not know how many of these analysts actually left the FBI for NCTC or other USIC partners, but observes that the mere notion that this many intelligence analysts were not considering a career at the FBI is alarming, and speaks to the need to make cultural changes that would encourage these analysts to stay. The Review Commission concludes that without an institutional recognition of the independent value of analysts' contributions, the Bureau will find it virtually impossible to complete its transformation to a domestic intelligence agency. Completing this transformation requires an experienced indigenous analytic cadre, and if the intent of FBI analysts serving at NCTC is any measure, building deep expertise and bench strength will not be achievable in a meaningful period of time with such potentially high rates of turnover.

(U) From DSOP's perspective, engagement and cooperation with the FBI has improved steadily over the past 10 years, with the Bureau a stronger player at the interagency level. The Review Commission surmises, however, that the FBI may no longer have a vested interest in the DSOP given the low number of its officers who are detailed there. Whereas the FBI had previously detailed a special agent and routinely sent entry-level officers to DSOP for the training experience, the FBI has apparently cut back significantly on the commitment of officers provided to DSOP, especially after sequestration. The few FBI officers currently serving in DSOP are intelligence analysts from the Counterterrorism Division (CTD). According to NCTC, the last year the FBI detailed a special agent to the DSOP was 2010.[292]

(U) The FBI-DOD Relationship

(U) The relationship between the DOD and FBI has historically been strongest when focused on specific missions requiring collaboration. The terrorist attacks of September 11, 2001, provided the impetus for building and strengthening the FBI-DOD partnership critical to counterterrorism and counterintelligence missions, and the aftermath of the Fort Hood shootings prompted a re-evaluation of DOD's and FBI's information sharing relationship. In the period of legal reform between 2001 and 2004, as the walls between law enforcement and intelligence were taken

---

290 (U) Ibid.
291 (U) Ibid.
292 (U) Ibid.

down, DOD and FBI built new bridges that enhanced intelligence cooperation, particularly in counterterrorism.[293]

(U) The Fort Hood shooting in November 2009 by Army Major Nidal Hasan caused the FBI to re-evaluate information sharing with the DOD within the JTTF structure. The Webster Commission found that the DOD and FBI were still operating under a 1979 information sharing MOU on counterintelligence activities that had only been amended in 1996, and an MOU that governed DOD participation in JTTFs that specifically prohibited broad information sharing with DOD outside of an FBI supervisor's approval.[294] As a result the FBI "did not share the Hasan information with any DOD employees other than the DCIS [Defense Criminal Investigative Service] and NCIS [Naval Criminal Investigative Service] personnel assigned to San Diego and WFO."[295] Moreover, the Webster Commission suggested that the FBI at the time preferred to assign leads relevant to DOD agencies to DOD JTTF TFOs, thereby introducing potential bias into the investigative process.[296]

(U) Immediately after the Fort Hood shooting, the FBI adopted a procedure requiring JTTFs to alert DOD and CTD formally if any individual with unique access to a military base, or with civilian or military status, became the subject of an FBI assessment or investigation.[297] Yet, the Webster Commission argued that this kind of information sharing procedure should be broadly implemented for law enforcement personnel and with other federal departments and agencies. The Webster Commission recommendation is consistent with the Review Commission's belief that JTTFs should implement formal procedures and best practices for information sharing that are not currently reflected in the standard MOUs governing JTTF participation. The Fort Hood shooting also prompted the DOD and FBI to pro-actively review and consolidate all of their 114 MOUs on information sharing into a single baseline MOU governing operational coordination and information sharing that was finalized in August 2011. Since 2011, the baseline MOU has been amended with specific annexes pertaining to DOD-FBI information sharing on counterterrorism, counterintelligence, terrorist screening, and other specifics pertaining to joint DOD-FBI partnerships.[298] The streamlining of DOD-FBI information sharing agreements is a useful illustration of the need for concise information sharing principles to govern information sharing between the Bureau and its partner agencies, and could be constructively applied to other partners, such as DHS.

---

293 (U) Three significant legal developments removed barriers to the FBI's information sharing relationship with the DOD between 2001 and 2004: the enactment of the USA PATRIOT Act of 2001 on October 26, 2001; the Intelligence Sharing Procedures for Foreign Intelligence and Foreign Counterintelligence Investigations Conducted by the FBI, issued by Department of Justice on March 6, 2002; and the Foreign Intelligence Surveillance Court of Review's November 18, 2002, opinion regarding the wall between intelligence and law enforcement on. Gary M. Bald, before the United States Senate Committee on the Judiciary, *Enhancing Information Sharing Initiatives,* September 21, 2005.

294 (U) *Webster Commission Report*, 25.

295 (U) *Webster Commission Report*, 73.

296 (U) *Webster Commission Report*, 78.

297 (U) *Webster Commission Report*, 94.

298 (U) See *Memorandum of Understanding between the Federal Bureau of Investigation and the Department of Defense Governing Information Sharing, Operational Coordination, and Investigative Responsibilities* and associated Annexes, August 2, 2011. For the justification for the MOU re-evaluation, see, August 2, 2011; 4-5.

(U) Currently, DOD and FBI have a robust program of joint duty rotations to and from FBI to support intelligence and operations. The FBI has several detailees assigned to DOD agencies in a non-intelligence capacity, which points to a healthy continuation of law enforcement relationships that pre-date September 11, 2001. A smaller number are assigned to DOD offices that produce intelligence. Unlike the CIA partnerships detailed previously, most of the intelligence analysts serving at DOD agencies are working in analytic positions at their gaining agency, which provides the FBI intelligence analysts with experience and expertise in intelligence production outside of the FBI.

(U) Former and current senior DOD intelligence officials we spoke to were largely positive on DIA's relationship with the FBI. The strength of the relationship between DIA and FBI seems largely the result of personal relationships that developed over a decade of sustained counterterrorism cooperation.[299] DOD senior officials were very positive on the partnership, which is focused on counterterrorism, and finds the FBI quite willing to collaborate. One official shared a concern, however, that not all reportable information finds its way into FBI intelligence reports, as FBI special agents are not accountable for reporting as much as they are for collection.[300]

(U) While the DIA-FBI relationship is quite strong, particularly on the human intelligence (HUMINT) side. DOD, in return, clearly values its partnership with FBI, as it has assigned numerous personnel to positions within the Bureau, most into USIC positions. One former DOD intelligence senior official claimed that he observed great progress under Director Mueller, particularly in the late 2000s, when he observed real advances in lateral communication and breaking down of internal stovepipes. Multiple current and former DOD intelligence officials commended the FBI for always being ready and willing to help and viewed the FBI and NSA counterterrorism partnership as outstanding, although ambiguity was acknowledged in the cyber arena among FBI, DHS, and NSA.[301]

(U) FBI-DOD Information Sharing Best Practices

(U) Three notable FBI-led organizations facilitate better joint operations between FBI and their defense and other counterparts: the High-Value Detainee Interrogation Group (HIG); the Terrorist Screening Center (TSC); and the FBI's Counterterrorism HUMINT Operations Unit (CHOU). Two of these have proven to be particularly successful models from the DOD perspective: the HIG and the CHOU.

(U) The HIG was formed under Presidential direction in 2010 to facilitate interviews of the highest value terrorist detainees as a complete interagency body under the administrative control

---

299 (U) See James Kitfield, "Flynn's Last Interview: Iconoclast departs DIA with a Warning," *Breaking Defense*, August 7, 2014 accessed at http://breakingdefense.com/2014/08/flynn's-last-interview-intel-iconoclast-departs-dia-with-a-warning/ (accessed on January 29, 2014). Comments by a former senior DOD official that DIA's "relationship and partnership with both the CIA and FBI are far stronger today than in the past, which is largely a result of the personal relationships we have established over the past decade of conflict."

300 (U) Memorandum for the Record, November 17, 2014.

301 (U) Memorandum for the Record, November 12, 2014.

of the FBI, with an FBI Director and two Deputy Directors, one from CIA and the other from DOD.[302] The HIG is an example of highly successful intelligence and law enforcement integration between the FBI and its USIC partners.[303]

(U) One of the most consistent information sharing and operational successes cited in the Review Commission's field office visits was the CHOU, established in October 2004 to enable FBI CHS to travel overseas and expand their bona fides or respond to critical intelligence community requirements in high-risk overseas operations.[304] CHOU began as a de-confliction program for joint source handling for CHSs in counterterrorism and directly supports field offices in collaboration with their interagency partners. CHOU's mission has since been expanded to coordinate and provide guidance and expertise of all FBI CT overseas CHS operations targeted against FBI collection priorities. The CHOU program has been so successful in enhancing and enabling critical operations that CTD believed the model should be exported to other operational divisions for joint source coordination, particularly in cyber, counterintelligence, and proliferation issues.[305] According to the FBI, to that end, the International Operations Division recently established a HUMINT Coordination Center within its Strategic Operations Unit to, among other things, streamline overseas source operations, accomplish deconfliction, and provide cross programmatic benefits to the LEGAT program and all divisions. The concept of a unit with comprehensive visibility into the overseas travel of CHSs connected to the operational divisions it supports is prudent in the Review Commission's view.[306] Moreover, the Review Commission believes that the CHOU is a best practice in USIC collaboration.

(U) The FBI-ODNI Relationship

(U) The DNI does not have the same ability to manage the resources of the domestic USIC elements as he does those that reside within the DOD, where long-standing agreements grant unambiguous authority over National Intelligence Program (NIP) funds to the DNI. Given that programmatic management is the primary tool the DNI has to ensure that intelligence investments are focused on national priorities and consistent with DNI standards and policies, the fact that the FBI has never been part of the core DOD NIP budget complicates its full integration into the USIC. The dearth of FBI assignees to the DNI staff in the early years of the ODNI and the unfamiliarity of most of the ODNI staff with the evolving legal regime for domestic collection initially reinforced the isolation of the FBI from the rest of the USIC.[307] Within the last five years, however, the FBI has begun to participate much more actively in community management activities on the ODNI staff. This participation has been enhanced by the FBI's

---

302 (U) *Final Charter for Operations of Interagency High-Value Detainee Interrogation Group (HIG Charter)*, April 22, 2010; Executive Order 13,491, Vol. 74 Fed. Reg. 4893, January 22, 2009.
303 (U) *HIG Charter; see, e.g., High-Value Detainee Interrogation Group Intelligence Highlights from Deployments*, October 16, 2013.
304 (U) Memorandum for the Record, October 21, 2014.
305 (U) Memorandum for the Record, October 21, 2014.
306 (U) Memorandum for the Record, November 14, 2014.
307 (U) Ibid.

91

increased collaboration with USIC partners, detailing out larger numbers of personnel to achieve these goals.[308]

(U) Senior ODNI staff and FBI personnel agree that integration with the USIC is continually improving. However, they agree that there is work still to be done to define how the FBI can help the DNI fulfill his broad mandate of conducting national intelligence.[309] A senior FBI official cited the reluctance of the ODNI to figure out how to leverage state and local knowledge in support of national security missions,[310] while one senior ODNI official cited the untapped potential of the Domestic DNI Representatives to contribute to national intelligence priorities.[311]

(U) In 2012, the DNI issued Intelligence Community Directive 402 creating 12 Domestic DNI Representatives, modeled on the roles of the COSs who perform this function at embassies overseas, and the roles of the DNI Representatives to DOD Combatant Commands. While the creation of the Domestic DNI Representatives is an important acknowledgment of the DNI's responsibilities in the Homeland and the primary role played by the Bureau in meeting those responsibilities, it is also clear that this program is experiencing growing pains. It is not well defined by the ODNI or well understood by the ADICs and SACs who serve in this capacity.[312] Some confusion stems from the question of which functions the ADIC/SAC is performing for the DNI as opposed to performing as part of his/her FBI responsibilities, because the stakeholder groups are not the same. Most ADICs/SACs understand that the Domestic DNI Representative role is to lead coordination, but are not clear what should be coordinated, and to what end. ADICs/SACs did not believe that they had adequate guidance on how to manage the Domestic DNI Representative responsibilities beyond their own field office's geographic area, given that some of the 12 regions are quite large.[313]

(U) One senior ODNI official expressed the belief that the Joint Regional Intelligence Group (JRIG) could have provided an organizational structure to undergird the Domestic DNI Representatives as they attempted to coordinate regional actions in response to USIC priorities. However, the JRIG program has been terminated and the FBI now supports the regional analytical capability within the existing FBI field office intelligence program. The high turnover also made it difficult for SACs to gain much traction in their new DNI role and manage their intelligence programs effectively.[314] Domestic DNI representatives, in conjunction with the ODNI staff and FBI Headquarters, could play a constructive role in promoting legal and appropriate collection and sharing of information on both national and local priorities, but that work needs to be done within a defined requirements and management framework that has not yet emerged. Much of what is happening in the field is driven by individuals with specific

---

308 (U) As of September 2014, several FBI personnel were serving in the ODNI. Memorandum for the Record, November 11, 2014. ; Memorandum for the Record, November 14, 2014. ; FBI/HRD/LEICLO data as of September 2014, Response to Request for Information, October 16, 2014. .
309 (U) Memorandum for the Record, November 11, 2014. ; Memorandum for the Record, November 14, 2014.
310 (U) Memorandum for the Record, November 21, 2014.
311 (U) Memorandum for the Record, November 11, 2014.
312 (U) Memorandum for the Record, July 21, 2014. ; Memorandum for the Record, July 30, 2014. ; Memorandum for the Record, November 11, 2014.
313 (U) Memorandum for the Record, July 30, 2014.
314 (U) Memorandum for the Record, November 21, 2014.

mission interests who can generate coalitions of the willing, and not by articulated national requirements.[315] This may result in the occasional product, but is not a way to consistently leverage the expertise in the field against the USIC's highest priorities. How the DNI's requirements framework intersects with the FBI's Threat Review and Prioritization Process must also be better defined—they will overlap, but should not necessarily be the same.

(U) The Review Commission recommends accelerating development of a systematic framework for identifying USIC requirements for the Homeland that the SAC/Domestic DNI Representatives can use to focus collaboration in the field. Additionally, the ODNI should provide policy guidance on how state and local law enforcement and other non-Title 50 elements in the Homeland can legally and appropriately intersect with the USIC via the Domestic DNI Representatives.

(U) Over and above its relationship with the ODNI, the FBI is the only intelligence agency charged with domestic intelligence. When it comes to collection in the Homeland that can identify and characterize emerging terrorist threats, the FBI is the key player. The FBI's missions, authorities, and history make it the most flexible and capable collector, particularly against US persons. Because of the unique role it plays in the Homeland, it is important that the FBI have the capability to identify new threats through its HUMINT collection and domain analysis, in addition to collecting against threats identified by foreign intelligence.

(U) As the FBI began its transformation into a national security organization, at the heart of that transformation was the concept of domain awareness. Domain awareness reflected the realization that the FBI could not be reactive and wait for cases to develop, it had to proactively seek to understand its environment. From the Review Commission's perspective, that means that domain analysis, which attempts to capture what is known and identify gaps for further collection, is at the heart of the FBI's transformation into a domestic intelligence agency, and it needs to be a process informed by everything the USIC has to offer. This includes all information from local sources—law enforcement, colleges and universities, and prisons—to which other parts of the USIC do not have access. Robust domain analysis will allow the FBI to harness its considerable skill at collection and source development in support of identifying new threats in addition to collecting against known threats. A failure to achieve that goal will leave the US with a domestic security service rather than a domestic intelligence agency, and with a vulnerability to homegrown threats that fall outside the purview of our foreign intelligence establishment.[316] As we have reviewed the FBI's progress towards this goal, it is clear that a great deal of progress has been made and that the FBI leadership understands what needs to be done and is committed to doing it. However, our field research, interviews, and document reviews have revealed weaknesses in analysis, HUMINT, and reporting that require focused attention if the FBI is to complete its transformation and integrate more fully with its USIC counterparts. As the FBI addresses these challenges, there is much the DNI and the USIC at large can do to help the FBI go the final distance to becoming both a threat-driven intelligence agency and an intelligence-driven law enforcement agency. Understandably, the things that remain to be done are hard, and will require a process for adapting best practices from the FBI's

---

315 (U) Memorandum for the Record, November 11, 2014.
316 (U) Memorandum for the Record, March 7, 2014.

more innovative field offices and from elements of the USIC that are recognized subject matter experts. These matters, as they pertain to emerging threats, were also addressed in Chapter III.

(U) The FBI-Private Sector Relationship

(U) The FBI engages with the private sector through InfraGard, the Business Alliance Council, the Higher Education Advisory Board, strategic partnership initiatives at individual field offices, membership in the Domestic Security Alliance Council (DSAC), established tripwire programs, and sector-focused initiatives (e.g., Maritime, Rail). These efforts are generally sponsored and overseen by different FBI Headquarters elements for different mission purposes and managed by different special agents in the field offices, albeit on a part-time basis. This creates a certain amount of outreach overlap in the field, with some private sector partners working with the FBI on counterintelligence, cyber, counterterrorism, and criminal issues, while also interacting with DHS because they are part of one of the 16 critical infrastructure sectors. In early 2014, the FBI created the position of Director of Private Sector Engagement to institute a broader and better integrated strategy for interfacing with the private sector but it is too early for the Review Commission to judge its effectiveness. Through this office, the FBI recently reviewed all of its private sector engagement programs in an effort to implement an overarching strategy through DSAC.

(U) There are ongoing efforts to improve and streamline Federal Government engagement with the private sector, including a pilot program being led by Cyber Division (CYD) to develop a new prototype for sharing information with private sector partners.[317] In its field office visits, the Review Commission heard some of the same complaints from industry partners that we heard from local law enforcement: information provided to the FBI is a one-way dialogue in that private sector partners never find out if that information was useful or acted upon. To address this issue, the FBI is increasing the number of outreach briefings provided to industry partners. The FBI is granting more, interim national security clearances to facilitate the sharing of classified information with corporate leaders concerning threats to their industries. We also heard from private sector partners that FBI and DHS do not appear to be coordinating their interactions with the private sector the same way they do their interactions with local law enforcement and from FBI agents frustrated to find DHS personnel on their way out as they are headed in to meet with an industry partner. DSAC now has DHS personnel collocated within its organization in its continuing effort to improve the partnership with DHS.

(U) As these interagency issues evolve, a common suggestion for improving the quality and consistency of its private sector partnerships is for the FBI to assign special agents at the field offices to be full-time liaisons. InfraGard's leadership and special agents in the field view the part-time coordinator positions as less than optimal, because to do more than respond to phone calls and have occasional meetings would require a full-time position—ideally filled by an experienced special agent. The Review Commission understands that most experienced special agents might not be enthusiastic about such a role because the position lacks the defined metrics associated with the prosecution of cases.[318] If the duties of multiple individuals who conduct

---

317 (U) Memorandum for the Record, September 29, 2014.
318 (U) Ibid.

part-time outreach to the private sector were combined into one full-time position, it would seem to provide a more efficient and effective approach but would also require additional coordination at FBI Headquarters and among the divisions to ensure all Bureau requirements were being met.

(U) The Review Commission learned that the FBI liaison positions have traditionally been undervalued but that has begun to change as more experienced special agents take on the role, although this has not yet resulted in adequate numbers of assigned special agents or adequate training for those in the position. One field office noted that it had 400 cleared defense contractors (CDCs) in its AOR—ranging from large well known names to far smaller enterprises—with only one liaison officer handling hundreds of CDCs. This field office emphasized the critical need for more liaison officers to conduct outreach to these companies to promote better internet hygiene, reduce the number of breaches, and promote long-term cooperation with the FBI.[319] Another field office noted, however, some sensitivity in these liaison relationships because labeling private sector contacts as sources could create a stigma. The field office argued that liaison contacts should be considered valuable and special agents should receive credit for the quality of liaison relationships the same way they do for CHSs.[320]

(U) The Review Commission supports the Director of Private Sector Engagement in bringing clarity to the FBI's interaction with the private sector. Still, the Review Commission was surprised to discover that the InfraGard relationship is still managed out of the CYD. InfraGard was first developed in 1996 to provide robust information sharing between public and private sector organizations to protect cyber infrastructure and equities. The program expanded in 1998 to become a nationally managed program by FBI Headquarters. In 2003, InfraGard program management was moved to Cyber Division, given the historical cyber focus of the partnerships in the field InfraGard has achieved good traction with industry and retains enough separation from the FBI to be viewed as an honest broker. It appears ready and willing to expand the liaison services it provides to the FBI.[321] The current limitations on InfraGard stem from the fact that InfraGard coordinators are part-time, and InfraGard is viewed as cyber-focused, when in fact it could have a broader portfolio. If InfraGard were to broaden its focus, however, it would make even more sense to realign it under the Director of Private Sector Engagement.

(U) The FBI and Countering Violent Extremism

(U) The FBI, like DHS, NCTC, and other agencies, has made an admirable effort to counter violent extremism (CVE) as mandated in the White House's December 2011 strategy, *Empowering Local Partners to Prevent Violent Extremism in the United States*. In January 2012, the FBI established the Countering Violent Extremism Office (CVEO) under the National Security Branch.[322] The CVEO was re-aligned in January 2013 to CTD's Domestic Terrorism Operations Section, under the National JTTF, to better leverage the collaborative participation of

---

319 (U) Memorandum for the Record, September 23, 2014.
320 (U) Memorandum for the Record, September 19, 2014.
321 (U) Memorandum for the Record, September 29, 2014.
322 (U) This was done in response to in response to the White House *Strategic Implementation Plan for Empowering Local Partners to Prevent Violent Extremism* (December 2011).

the dozens of participating agencies in FBI's CVE efforts.[323] Yet, even within FBI, there is a misperception by some that CVE efforts are the same as FBI's community outreach efforts. Many field offices remain unaware of the CVE resources available through the CVEO.[324] Because the field offices have to own and integrate the CVE portfolio without the benefit of additional resources from FBI Headquarters, there is understandably inconsistent implementation. The Review Commission, through interviews and meetings, heard doubts expressed by FBI personnel and its partners regarding the FBI's central role in the CVE program. The implementation had been inconsistent and confusing within the FBI, to outside partners, and to local communities.[325] The CVEO's current limited budget and fundamental law enforcement and intelligence responsibilities do not make it an appropriate vehicle for the social and prevention role in the CVE mission. Such initiatives are best undertaken by other government agencies. The Review Commission recommends that the primary social and prevention responsibilities for the CVE mission should be transferred from the FBI to DHS or distributed among other agencies more directly involved with community interaction.

(U) Conclusion

(U) The Review Commission finds that the FBI has made real and significant progress in information sharing and collaboration, particularly given the challenges of doing so across such a large, decentralized, and globally dispersed organization. The FBI has developed a constructive partnership with DHS, and the relationships the FBI has forged with key USIC partners such as CIA, NCTC, NSA, and DIA, are excellent and improving. The FBI has become a key player on the ODNI staff, and is integrating more into the USIC, although the separation of its budget from the bulk of the DOD NIP continues to be a limiting factor.

(U) To address the 9/11 Commission's mandate concerning collaboration and information sharing with state and local authorities and the private sector, the FBI should focus on the JTTFs and engagement with the private sector: ensuring the right agencies are represented in JTTFs; ensuring JTTF TFOs have the same access to information as their FBI counterparts; developing policies on when and what types of information should be shared with local authorities; developing ways to provide feedback to state and local law enforcement and private sector partners; and increasing and clarifying liaison with the private sector.

(U) Findings and Recommendations

(U) Overall, the FBI has made substantial progress in building collaborative relationships with its key partners across the US Government. These relationships have improved cooperation and information sharing. Nonetheless, the Review Commission notes that the pace of such progress can neither decrease nor stall in light of an uncertain future characterized by dramatic changes in the threats facing the United States. Most importantly, the FBI should set a goal of improving

---

323 (U) See *FBI Strategic Plan to Curb Violent Extremism* (Undated).
324 (U) Ibid.
325 (U) See FBI, National Security Branch, *Countering Violent Extremism Office Communications Strategy*, August 2013: 2.

partner relationships to further increase the speed and volume of intelligence information it exchanges with the USIC and law enforcement.

(U) Finding 1: FBI special agents and supervisors appear to share a widespread perception that the Justice Department's NSD is overly bureaucratic and insufficiently aggressive in reviewing and approving requests for authorization and/or FISA warrants.

(U) Recommendation 1: The Review Commission recommends FBI ADICS/SACs be briefed on procedural review requirements, as well as reasonable anticipated timelines, for investigative activities to be approved by NSD. The Justice Department's NSD should be requested to provide a review and approval timeline so that the FBI will have realistic expectations of how quickly a FISA warrant may be reviewed and submitted for approval by the FISC.

(U) Finding 2: The JTTF is an effective and essential element in the post-9/11 counterterrorism environment, but the structure and composition of the JTTFs are too variable. TFOs within the JTTFs still do not consistently have access to all necessary data, and SACs would benefit from more transparent guidelines regarding what information should be shared with state and local partners.

(U) Recommendation 2: The Review Commission recommends that the FBI evaluate the JTTF's policies and procedures to determine a more standard approach to strengthen the JTTFs.

- (U) The Review Commission recommends that the FBI take immediate action to resolve, by system modifications, policy, and/or training, the issues that prevent TFOs from having full access to Guardian, Sentinel, and any other information sources needed for them to operate as equal members of the Task Force and to be cognizant of information relevant to their home organization. Most importantly, the solutions should include mechanisms to alert both TFOs and their FBI supervisors when something has changed that affects database access so that corrective action can be taken.

- (U) The Review Commission recommends that the FBI develop policy guidelines that continue to respect the judgment of the ADIC/SAC but provide a framework within which to make decisions regarding real-time sharing of information with key local partners under defined circumstances. The implementation of this guidance should be included in regular field training exercises that include FBI and local law enforcement.

(U) Finding 3: The FBI's engagement with, and commitment to, the fusion centers and their component entities across the United States is uneven. The Review Commission acknowledges that this reflects, in part, a conscious decision by the Bureau to gauge the appropriate level of interaction with each fusion center. That said, a consistent refrain from the FBI's partners in the fusion centers is the desire for more feedback on information provided to the FBI. These partners recognize that the FBI may be limited in what feedback it can provide, but also maintain that a one-way partnership is fragile and problematical. The FBI is widely viewed as sharing information when it serves an immediate FBI purpose, and not for thinking systemically about building relationships for the future through information sharing.

(U) Recommendation 3: The Review Commission recommends that the FBI address the lingering perceptions among state and local law enforcement and other partners that it views relationships as transactional and tactical and is not interested in building lasting partnerships that advance common goals and missions; the Bureau should develop a strategy to address such perceptions head on.

- (U) In view of the above, the Review Commission recommends that the FBI continue to exploit advanced technology to ensure that state and local law enforcement get timely and useful feedback.

- (U) The Review Commission also recommends that for private sector organizations, the FBI design a process to give feedback on information they have received from these organizations that does not compromise sensitive information owing to privacy considerations or ongoing investigations. The FBI should be more transparent in explaining the reasons why it may not be able to provide such feedback to private sector organizations on information they have provided.

(U) Finding 4: The FBI and the DNI need to work together to make the Domestic DNI Representative program a more meaningful contributor to meeting the needs of US national security domestically. The program is poorly understood in the field and lacks a common requirements framework to make it useful to the ODNI.

(U) Recommendation 4: The Review Commission recommends that the FBI work with the DNI to establish a framework for engaging and managing the Domestic DNI Representative program.

- (U) As part of this framework, the FBI should clarify—in consultation with the DNI—the rules of engagement with state and local and other federal partners who are not in the USIC but who may contribute valuable information to its domain knowledge.

- (U) The Review Commission recommends that new ADIC/SACs through enhanced training develop a broader understanding of the USIC, national-level intelligence requirements as they relate to the FBI, and the role of the Domestic DNI Representatives before they take their posts.

(U) Finding 5: The FBI—along with NSA, Cyber Command, and DHS—plays a key role in anticipating and protecting US cyber security. The FBI's relationship with the private sector, in turn, is of increasing importance to its ability to address cyber threats. But the FBI's engagement with the private sector remains fragmented.

(U) Recommendation 5: The Review Commission recommends that the FBI enhance and accelerate its outreach to the private sector.

- (U) The FBI should work with Congress to develop legislation that facilitates private companies' communication and collaboration and work with the US Government in countering cyber threats.

- (U) The FBI should play a prominent role in coordinating with the private sector, which the Review Commission believes will require a full-time position for a qualified special agent in the relevant field offices, as well as existing oversight at Headquarters.

(U) Finding 6: The CVEO's current limited budget and fundamental law enforcement and intelligence responsibilities do not make it an appropriate vehicle for the social and prevention role in the CVE mission. Such initiatives are best undertaken by other government agencies.

(U) Recommendation 6: The Review Commission recommends that the primary social and prevention responsibilities for the CVE mission should be transferred from the FBI to DHS or distributed among other agencies more directly involved with community interaction.

CHAPTER V
(U) NEW INFORMATION RELATED TO THE 9/11 ATTACKS

(U) The 9/11 Commission noted in its final report that it had "endeavored to provide the most complete account of the events of September 11" but conceded nonetheless that "[n]ew information will inevitably come to light."[326] Consistent with this, the Review Commission's congressional mandate included an "assessment of any evidence now known to the FBI that was not considered by the 9/11 Commission related to any factors that contributed in any manner to the terrorist attacks of September 11, 2001."[327]

(U) To fulfill this mandate, the Review Commission conducted multiple interviews of key personnel at FBI Headquarters and in the field to identify any new information related to the 9/11 attacks, with a special emphasis on identifying any previously unknown co-conspirators. The Review Commission traveled to the New York and San Diego field offices to speak with FBI personnel who have continued to investigate the 9/11 attacks and received briefings at FBI Headquarters from several of the lead investigators and analysts on new evidence that has come to light since the 9/11 Commission's 2004 report. Finally, the Review Commission made requests for information specifically on possible links between the San Diego-based hijackers, Nawaf al-Hazmi and Khalid al-Mihdhar, as well as the pre-9/11 activities of Anwar al-Aulaqi. Given the time and resources available, it was beyond the scope of the Review Commission's activities to re-interview every witness or to review all of the documents related to the FBI's investigation of the 9/11 attacks. The FBI's investigation since 9/11 has involved over 500,000 leads, over 167,000 interviews, and millions of pages of documents.[328]

(U) The Review Commission found that the FBI, to its credit, still has the 9/11 attacks and any potential conspiracy surrounding them, under active investigation. The Review Commission also investigated two claims of allegedly new evidence reported in the press—an FBI source with purported access to Usama bin Laden (UBL) in the early 1990s and a Sarasota family that was alleged to have suspiciously left the United States shortly before the 9/11 attacks. This chapter captures and reviews the results of the Review Commission's inquiry into these four topics.

---

326 (U) *The 9/11 Commission Report*, xvii.
327 (U) Public Law 113-6 and 113-76. (2013-2014); statement of Chairman Barbara Mikulski, *Congressional Record*, March 11, 2013: S1305.
328 (U) FBI Briefing, *Overview of 9/11 Investigation*, April 25, 2014.

(U) Key Points

- (U) Based on the available information obtained and considered, the Review Commission concludes that there is no new information to date that would alter the original findings of the 9/11 Commission regarding the individuals responsible for the 9/11 attacks or for supporting those responsible for the attacks.

- (U) There is new evidence, however, that confirms and strengthens the cases against previously known co-conspirators who are awaiting trial.

- (U) The Review Commission also concludes that media reports regarding a possible FBI source with access to UBL in the early 1990s or suspicions regarding a Saudi family resident in Sarasota before the 9/11 attacks did not hold up under scrutiny.

- (U) The Review Commission commends the FBI for continuing its active investigation into the 9/11 attacks.

(U) FBI Investigations

(U) The FBI's initial investigation into the 9/11 attacks was named PENTTBOM. This effort remains open and active. Subsequent to the initial 9/11 Commision report, the FBI opened a subfile within this investigation to sharpen the focus on the lingering allegations that the circle of 9/11 conspirators may be wider. The 9/11 Review Commission reviewed the status of both the PENTTBOM and subfile teams.

(U) Key Individuals In This Chapter

Nawaf al-Hazmi: 9/11 hijacker on Flight 77 who spent time in San Diego in 2000.

Khalid al-Mihdhar: 9/11 hijacker on Flight 77 who spent time in San Diego in 2000.

Omar al-Bayoumi: Manager of Kurdish Community Islamic Center (KCIC). Assisted al-Hazmi and al-Mihdhar as well as al-Sadhan and al-Sudairy during their respective times in San Diego.

Fahad al-Thumairy: Imam at the King Fahad mosque near Los Angeles and accredited diplomat at the Saudi consulate in Los Angeles who met al-Hazmi and al-Mihdhar.

Mohdhar Abdullah: Befriended and provided assistance to al-Hazmi and al-Mihdhar during their time in San Diego.

Khalid Sheik Mohammed (KSM): Mastermind of the 9/11 attacks.

(U) The 9/11 Commission detailed how al-Hazmi and al-Mihdhar arrived in Los Angeles in January 2000, but evidence regarding their initial activities was still incomplete. The 9/11 Commission inquired into whether Fahad al Thumairy—an imam at the King Fahad mosque in

Los Angeles and an accredited diplomat at the Saudi Arabian consulate from 1996 until 2003—"may have played a role in helping the hijackers establish themselves on their arrival in Los Angeles."[329] Based on the evidence available at the time, the 9/11 Commission concluded that there was no evidence that al-Thumairy provided assistance to al-Hazmi and al-Mihdhar.[330]

(U) The 9/11 Commission further considered the support that Omar al-Bayoumi provided to the hijackers and the circumstances of their meeting on February 1, 2000, at a restaurant in Culver City, a few blocks from the King Fahad mosque.[331] Despite a number of questions regarding al-Bayoumi's version of the events that day—particularly that he accidently encountered al-Hazmi and al-Mihdhar in the restaurant after overhearing their Gulf Arabic accents—coupled with his assistance to the hijackers after they moved to San Diego at his suggestion, the 9/11 Commission nonetheless concluded that al-Bayoumi was "an unlikely candidate for clandestine involvement with Islamist extremists."[332]

(U) In a July 2004 summary of its investigation into al-Bayoumi the FBI similarly determined that "evidence and intelligence do not indicate that al-Bayoumi had advance knowledge of the terrorist attacks of 9/11/2001 or knowledge of al-Hazmi's and/or al-Mihdhar's status as Al Qaeda operatives" or "that the assistance provided by al-Bayoumi to al-Hazmi and al-Mihdhar was witting."

(U) The 9/11 Commission also detailed that Mohdar Abdullah was a close associate of al-Hazmi and al-Mihdhar when they lived in San Diego. Abdullah denied knowing of the attacks in advance but the 9/11 Commission reported that Abdullah was aware of al-Hazmi and al-Mihdhar's extremist views and al-Mihdhar's involvement with the Islamic Army of Aden. Abdullah himself sympathized with those views.[333] In May 2004, the 9/11 Commission learned that Abdullah had reportedly bragged to fellow inmates that he had known in advance of al-Hazmi and al-Mihdhar's plans to conduct a terrorist attack.[334] There are various accounts of the alleged bragging and neither the FBI nor the 9/11 Commission was able to confirm the veracity of this new information.[335] The 9/11 Commission heard some speculation that al-Hazmi had called Abdullah in late August 2001 and leaked information that "something big was going to happen."[336] The 9/11 Commission did not in the end identify Abdullah as a witting supporter of the hijackers.

(U) The subfile team began its review of several individuals of interest in 2007. In describing its work to the Review Commission, the team identified the collection of information it had

---

329 (U) *The 9/11 Commission Report*, 216.
330 (U) Ibid., 217. A 2012 FBI summary of the status of the effort reported, however, that al-Thumairy "immediately assigned an individual to take care of al-Hazmi and al-Mihdhar during their time in the Los Angeles area."
331 (U) *The 9/11 Commission Report*, 217.
332 (U) *The 9/11 Commission Report*, 217-18.
333 (U) *The 9/11 Commission Report*, 218.
334 (U) Abdullah was detained in an immigration facility after pleading guilty to immigration charges for fraudulently claiming he was a Somali asylee.
335 (U) *The 9/11 Commission Report*, 218-19.
336 (U) *The 9/11 Commission Report*, 249.

reviewed. The majority of the materials, including those obtained from a New Scotland Yard search of al-Bayoumi's London apartment in late 2001, had been received by the FBI before the 9/11 Commission issued its report. The only new evidence came from re-interviews of specific individuals. For example, the FBI had interviewed Mohdar Abdullah on several occasions prior to the 9/11 Commission's 2004 report and then in 2007 and 2008. During a 2011 interview Abdullah confirmed that he had provided on his own accord various types of assistance to the hijackers in San Diego. He also reiterated that he had discussions with al-Hazmi regarding the latter's jihadist beliefs but said he did not believe that al-Hazmi was saying they should be terrorists. Abdullah also denied telling his cellmates that he had advance knowledge of the 9/11 attacks. The Review Commission did not discover anything new in the post-9/11 Commission interviews of Abdullah that would definitively change the 9/11 Commission's conclusions regarding Abdullah's pre-9/11 activities.

(U) Finding: The Review Commission finds that this new information is not sufficient to change the 9/11 Commission's original findings regarding the presence of witting assistance to al-Hazmi and al-Mihdhar. The Review Commission notes that there is ongoing internal debate within the FBI between the original PENTTBOM team and the subfile team regarding the potential significance of some of this information. The Review Commission recognizes the importance of strong internal engagement between the PENTTBOM and the subfile teams. The Review Commission recommends that the FBI leadership review both perspectives and continue the investigation accordingly.

(U) Guantanamo Bay Trial Preparation

(U) The second effort devoted to uncovering new evidence involves the trial preparations for the al-Qa'ida defendants currently held at Guantanamo Bay. This effort focuses on examination of materials obtained both pre- and post-2004, including materials from the Abbottabad raid, search warrants, and the recorded conversations of key individuals. None of this evidence identifies any additional participants in the planning or carrying out of the 9/11 attacks. This evidence does strengthen and enhance the cases against existing plotters.[337]

(U) Finding: The Review Commission finds that this new evidence further substantiates and strengthens previously known connections between hijackers and other plotters and reinforces the cases against them.[338]

(U) Alleged FBI Source with Access to Usama bin Laden

(U) On February 25, 2014, the *Washington Times* reported that the FBI had "placed a human source in direct contact with Osama bin Laden in 1993 and ascertained that the al Qaeda leader was looking to finance terrorist attacks in the United States."[339] The article claimed to be

---

337 (U) Memorandum for the Record, October 24, 2014.
338 (U) Ibid.
339 (U) Guy Taylor and John Solomon, "EXCLUSIVE: FBI had human source in contact with bin Laden as far back as 1993," *Washington Times,* February 25, 2014, http://www.washingtontimes.com/news/2014/feb/25/fbi-source-had-contact-with-osama-bin-ladin-in-1993 (accessed on November 19, 2014).

derived from the courtroom testimony of a Supervisory Special Agent, who in the 1990s was in charge of a counterterrorism squad in the Los Angeles Field Office, on which Special Agent Bassem Youssef worked. Youssef had developed the confidential source referenced in the *Washington Times* article. According to the witness, Youssef's source was close with Omar Abdel-Rahman, a radical Egyptian cleric living in the United States known as the "Blind Sheik," who was subsequently convicted on terrorist charges arising from the 1993 bombing of New York City's World Trade Center. The *Washington Times* reported that the witness, Youssef's former supervisor, testified that Youssef arranged to have the source travel overseas to meet personally with UBL and that UBL "had a target [a Masonic lodge] picked out for an explosion in the Los Angeles area."[340]

(U) The Review Commission interviewed Youssef. He said that "99 percent of the story was accurate."[341] He explained that from late 1992 to early 1993, Abdel-Rahman was "spewing anti-Egypt stuff at the mosque" but was not calling for attacks in or against the United States. In 1993, Youssef identified an individual, the aforementioned confidential source, who was in frequent contact with Abdel-Rahman—but not directly with UBL. Youssef learned from the source's wife and from two other informants about a plot to bomb a Masonic Lodge in Los Angeles "because it was frequented by Jews."[342] The plotters had sought Abdel-Rahman's approval who, in granting it, had mentioned in passing that "when they wanted to do something overseas," they should "talk to Usama" in order to obtain financing.[343] At the time, Abdel-Rahman was one of UBL's spiritual advisers. According to Youssef, he reported to FBI Headquarters in 1994 that "UBL is building an Islamic army, has a lot of money, and is charismatic" but, according to Youssef, UBL was not at that stage known to be "a criminal or a terrorist."[344] This is consistent with other, contemporaneous, USIC assessments.[345] With respect to the plot against the Masonic Lodge, Youssef stated that it had nothing to do with either UBL or al-Qa'ida and, in any event, never materialized. Moreover, the source in question was in fact in direct contact with Abdel-Rahman, and not directly with UBL. Youssef said that the source was killed while fighting in Chechnya in 1995.[346]

(U) The Review Commission also reviewed an affidavit dated March 11, 2014, provided for the same trial that was described in the *Washington Times* account. The affiant, a Supervisory Special Agent currently assigned to the Los Angeles Field Office, stated that he had recently reviewed Youssef's source files from the 1990s. The affidavit confirmed that Youssef first met the confidential source in June 1993 and recruited him as a source two months later. The

---

340 (U) Ibid. The actual testimony is less clear. The Supervisory Special Agent actually testified, "[Youssef] was able to develop two sources that were directly involved with Abdel Rahman. . .. [T]he one source came back, had direct contact with Osama bin Laden. He had indicated to Abdel Rahman that he had a target picked out for an explosion in the Los Angeles area, I believe it was a Masonic lodge. Abdel Rahman went and told him to go get money from Usama back in the Middle East." See Testimony of Edward Curran, *Bassam Youssef* vs. *Federal Bureau of Investigation, et. al.*, CA No. 03-1551 (September 15, 2010). It is unclear to whom the term "he" refers.
341 (U) Memorandum for the Record, November 10, 2014.
342 (U) Ibid.
343 (U) Ibid.
344 (U) Ibid.
345 (U) John Miller and Michael Stone, *The Cell* (New York: Hyperion, 2002): 137-138.
346 (U) Memorandum for the Record, November 10, 2014.

affidavit states that "There is no evidence in any of the files that Youssef's source had direct contact with Osama bin Laden. Nor is there any evidence that Youssef's source directly implicated Osama bin Laden in funding and planning a terrorist attack in Los Angeles or elsewhere in the United States." He further recounted how the source underwent two polygraphs, both of which indicated deception. Furthermore, Youssef had documented in the file that the source was unreliable. The affidavit also confirmed that Youssef had lost contact with the source in July 1994 and never was in communication with him again. He further confirmed that there was no information in the source file regarding al-Qa'ida and that Youssef had specifically recorded in the file that the source was not within al-Qa'ida.[347]

(U) There appear to be small inconsistencies between Youssef's recollection of events from two decades ago and the more recent affidavit but Youssef confirmed that the source had not in fact been in direct contact with UBL. Even if the source had actually been in direct contact with UBL in the less than a year he was an FBI intelligence asset, any information the source may or may not have had regarding UBL would certainly have provided no indication of the September 11, 2001, plot—the planning of which did not commence until late 1998 or early 1999.[348] In any event, it was not until the 1998 attacks on the US embassies in Africa that the United States would see an attack "planned, directed, and executed by al Qaeda, under the direct supervision of bin Laden and his chief aides" and the 9/11 Commission concluded that UBL's involvement in the 1993 World Trade Center bombing was "at best cloudy."[349]

(U) It should also be noted that the FBI case against UBL was opened in October 1995, a year after Youssef had lost contact with the confidential source and apparently after the source was already dead.[350] Moreover, based on the affidavit, there was apparently nothing in the source file that would have led the New York special agents investigating UBL to believe that Youssef's source might be of interest to their investigation.[351]

(U) **Finding:** The Commission finds that the existence of an FBI confidential source who may or may not have had the ability to contact UBL directly in 1993-94 has no relevance to the 9/11 Commission's final conclusions on the 9/11 attacks.

(U) The Sarasota Family

(U) On September 8, 2011, the *Broward Bulldog*, an online local investigative newspaper, reported that the FBI allegedly had "found troubling ties between the hijackers and residents in an upscale community" near Sarasota, Florida. The article claimed that two weeks before the 9/11 attacks, members of a Saudi family "abruptly left their luxury home" leaving behind their cars, furniture, a refrigerator full of food, clothes, and other goods.[352] An unidentified

---

347 (U) Declaration Of Christopher Castillo (Castillo Declaration) submitted in the case of *Bassem Youssef* vs. *Eric Holder, Jr. Attorney General.*, Case No. 03-CV-1551 (March 11, 2014).
348 (U) *The 9/11 Commission Report*, 154.
349 (U) Ibid., 59 and 67.
350 (U) *The Cell*: 148.
351 (U) *Castillo Declaration*.
352 (U) Anthony Summers and Dan Christensen, "FBI Found Direct Ties Between 911 Hijackers and Saudis Living in Florida; Congress Kept in Dark," *The Broward Bulldog*, September, 2011.

"counterterrorism officer" was quoted as saying that phone records and the community gate records "linked the house on Escondito Circle to the hijackers."[353] The article purported that this information had not been shared with Congress or mentioned in the 9/11 Commission Report.[354]

(U) A subsequent article in the *Miami Herald*, referring to an FBI document that had been produced pursuant to a Freedom of Information Act request, reported that the FBI document indicated that "[a] Saudi family who 'fled' their Sarasota area home weeks before 9/11 had 'many connections' to 'individuals associated with the terrorist attacks on 9/11/2001'."[355] The FBI told the Review Commission that the FBI Electronic Communication (EC) on which the news article was based was "poorly written" and wholly unsubstantiated. When questioned later by others in the FBI, the special agent who wrote the EC was unable to provide any basis for the contents of the document or explain why he wrote it as he did.[356]

(U) The Review Commission requested and received a briefing regarding the press allegations. The Review Commission also obtained a copy of the case file, copies of documents released through the Freedom of Information Act regarding the matter, and reports of interviews.

(U) The FBI informed the Review Commission that contrary to the contents of the original EC cited by the *Miami Herald,* the FBI had in fact "found no evidence that connected the family members in the *Miami Herald* article to any of the 9/11 hijackers, nor was there any connection found between the family and the 9/11 plot."[357] The FBI explained to the Review Commission that following the 9/11 attacks the Bureau received numerous calls from the public to report suspicious activity.

(U) The FBI followed up on these initial leads in September 2001. Over several years, the FBI interviewed numerous individuals with direct knowledge of the facts forming the basis of the reports of suspicious activity. These individuals included all of the relevant family members and local individuals who claimed to have, or the FBI believed might have, pertinent information. The FBI also conducted an extensive review of records which might have contained pertinent information. The FBI found that the alleged derogatory information was unsubstantiated. The leads were determined to be covered and no further action was needed.

(U) The FBI told the Review Commission that the EC was apparently based solely on unsubstantiated reports from others and there was no documentation supporting its allegations.

---

http://www.browardbulldog.org/2011/09/fbi-found-direct-ties-between -911-hijackers-amd-Saudis-living-in-Florida-congress-kept-in-dark (accessed on December 12, 2014).
353 (U) Ibid.
354 (U) Ibid.
355 (U) Anthony Summers and Dan Christensen, "FBI Report: Florida Family Had Ties to People Linked to 9/11 Attacks," *The Miami Herald*, April 17, 2011 http://miamiherald.com/incoming/article1950334.html (accessed on May 1, 2014). See also, April 16, 2002.
356 (U) Memorandum for the Record, April 30, 2014.
357 (U) Ibid.

After further investigation, the FBI determined that the statements in the EC were incorrect.[358] The FBI found no evidence of contact, between the hijackers and the family.[359]

(U) Finding: The allegations that the family was connected to the hijackers and/or the 9/11 plot were not substantiated. A review of the complete record demonstrated that the newspaper articles were based on inaccurate information and a poorly written and innaccurate FBI EC.

(U) Overall Finding: The FBI has continued to investigate the 9/11 attacks; however, no new information obtained since the 9/11 Commission 2004 report would change the 9/11 Commission's findings regarding responsibilities for the 9/11 attacks. And contrary to media reports, the FBI did not have a source in the early 1990s with direct access to UBL nor was there credible evidence linking the Sarasota, Florida, family to the hijackers.

(U) Recommendation: The 9/11 Review Commission recommends the FBI continue its thorough investigation into the 9/11 attacks and, after the trials of the conspirators conclude, capture the lessons learned through the investigation, and provide detailed briefings to Director Comey and the relevant congressional oversight committees.

---

358 (U) Memorandum for the Record, April 30, 2014.
359 (U) Memorandum for the Record, April 30, 2014.

(U) KEY FINDINGS AND RECOMMENDATIONS

(U) In the post-9/11 world, threats are defined more by the fault lines
within societies than by the territorial boundaries between them.
From terrorism to global disease or environmental degradation,
the challenges have become transnational rather than international.
That is the defining quality of world politics in the twenty-first century.[360]
-The 9/11 Commission Report

(U) The Threat

(U) Finding 1: Over the past decade, the Bureau has made measurable progress building a threat-based, intelligence driven-national security organization. In the same period, however, global threats to the US Homeland have become more complex, challenging the FBI's traditional orientation as the primary federal law enforcement organization, its change-resistant culture, and its core capabilities in criminal investigation, counterintelligence, intelligence collection and analysis, and technology.

- (U) Fueled by the spread of new technology and social media as well as and hostile states and transnational networks, which include terrorists, "lone wolves," returning foreign fighters, cyber hackers and organized syndicates, weapons of mass destruction (WMD) proliferators, narcotics and human traffickers, and other organized criminals are increasingly operating against US interests across national borders.

(U) Recommendation 1: The FBI needs to accelerate the pace of its reforms and transformation of its culture to counter these dynamic threats and fulfill its expanding global mission as a fully integrated, intelligence-driven investigative organization under visional leadership and enabled by state-of-the-art technology.

(U) Improving Intelligence Analysis and Collection

(U) Finding 2: The Review Commission believes that the Intelligence Branch (IB) has an essential role to play within the FBI and throughout the United States Intelligence Community (USIC). During our review, we found that the FBI has made progress in building the framework to support its intelligence function but continues to lag in capability. We are concerned about whether or not the IB's Strategic Plan and Program of Analysis will deliver enhanced subject matter expertise in an acceptable timeframe to address the rapidly evolving threats.

- (U) The Bureau, despite its stated intentions to address the concerns of its intelligence analysts, still does not sufficiently recognize them as a professionalized workforce with distinct requirements for investment in training and education, rotational opportunities

---

360 (U) *The 9/11 Commission Report: Final Report of the National Commission on Terrorist Attacks Upon the United States* (New York: W.W. Norton & Company, 2004): 362.

across the USIC, and a career service that will meet both the professional expectations of analysts and the growing needs of a global service.

(U) Recommendation 2: The Review Commission views its recommendation to enhance the analyst career service as a top priority among the following other proposals to improve analysis, collection, and training for both analysts and special agents:

- (U) The career service, led by the Executive Assistant Director (EAD) for Intelligence, should incorporate analyst managers at senior levels throughout the Bureau and the USIC. It should establish standards for training and education (and access to it) and for periodic rotations to other agencies.

- (U) The career service should set criteria for promotions based on the mastery of explicit analytic skills. The FBI should provide appropriate incentives for subject matter experts. The Review Commission strongly recommends that a group of outside experts be convened to monitor the progress of this career service.

- (U) The Bureau should implement changes to demonstrate its value as an intelligence workforce, including staffing the IB organization with more intelligence professionals.

- (U) The analysts should be further trained and incentivized to do strategic and domain analysis, supporting criminal investigation, national intelligence priorities, and the requirements from other agencies. To accomplish this, they must be empowered and equipped with cutting edge technology, desk-top connectivity to the USIC, and strong local incentives that encourage special agent and analyst collaboration to produce forward-looking, integrated domain analysis and collection plans. This must be at the highest priority for FBI leadership at all levels.

- (U) Leadership should focus on building the domain analytic capability at the field office level, including tradecraft development, improved access to information, increased analytic collaboration between Headquarters and the field, and enhanced training.

- (U) The FBI must improve the Human Intelligence (HUMINT) program with greater emphasis on the integration of analytic, technical, and national-intelligence resources; HUMINT and operational squads should collectively identify gaps and mitigation strategies; and established metrics for this program should institute career tracks and reward innovative thinking and efforts towards identifying new threats.

- (U) The Bureau should provide consistent managerial guidance for the staff operations specialist (SOS) career field, as well as a codified path that allows for transition into other professional roles.

- (U) Training should be provided to new Special Agent in Charge (SACs), prior to assuming their posts, on current or new national-level intelligence requirements as they relate to the FBI and to the role of the Domestic Director of National Intelligence (DNI) Representatives.

- (U) The Review Commission recommends FBI Assistant Directors in Charge (ADICS)/SACs be briefed on procedural review requirements, as well as reasonable anticipated timelines, for investigative activities to be approved by the National Security Division (NSD). The Justice Department's NSD should be requested to provide a review and approval timeline so that the FBI will have realistic expectations of how quickly a Foreign Intelligence Surveillance Act (FISA) warrant may be reviewed and submitted for approval by the Foreign Intelligence Surveillance Court (FISC).

- (U) The requirements for intelligence collection and analysis should be more fully reflected in consistent and clearly defined criteria for inspections at field offices and Headquarters.

(U) Leadership

(U) Finding 3: Leadership at all levels of the FBI is not unified or consistent in driving cultural change. The workforce grasps the FBI's stated intention to transform itself into an intelligence-driven, threat-based agency, but implementation varies widely.

- (U) The Review Commission interviewed leaders at Headquarters and in the field, who were all committed to the Bureau's mission as they see it, but who, in their comments and demeanor, range from high-energy change agents to passive resistors regarding the pursuit of an integrated intelligence and law enforcement mission.

- (U) The frequent turnover of leadership seriously hampers the pace of reform.

(U) Recommendation 3: Director Comey has continued the focus on strategic leadership that was a cornerstone of the transformation initiated by former Director Mueller. The Review Commission recommends that the Director continue to explore all options and flexibility to retain senior leaders for longer tours at Headquarters and in the field. The Director should work with Congress and the Office of Personnel Management to develop options for leadership retention.

- (U) The Review Commission further recommends that the Director closely involve his rising leaders in the development of a strategic vision for the Bureau with explicit goals that can be communicated by leadership throughout the organization. Investment in strategic leadership training, both internal and external, should be significantly increased at all levels.

- (U) Performance reviews should evaluate leaders on the basis of their ability to communicate and implement the Director's strategic goals.

(U) Integration

(U) Finding 4: The FBI today is not sufficiently integrated into the USIC, despite the potential to improve support to its own criminal investigations and to fill critical intelligence gaps for the USIC. Well-conceived programs intended to boost intelligence capacity, such as HUMINT squads and Central Strategic Coordinating Components (CSCC), struggle in the field in part because of local leadership choices amid competing threats.

(U) Recommendation 4: The FBI Director should, for the benefit of FBI intelligence personnel, work closely with the DNI and USIC agency heads to increase and sustain interagency collaboration in training rotational assignments, and project related working opportunities. He also should accelerate the acquisition of Sensitive Compartmental Information Facilities (SCIF) space and analyst tools to facilitate the Bureau's integration into the USIC.

- (U) The FBI Director and the DNI should work together to make the Domestic DNI Representative program a more meaningful contributor to meeting the needs of US national security domestically.

- (U) The FBI must better use its strategic processes to drive the intelligence cycle for its law enforcement and intelligence missions. The two missions should operate in concert, utilizing the intelligence cycle to inform and drive investigations. The FBI should sustain its commitment to the integration into the USIC common desktop environment, applications mall, and back-office design.

- (U) The FBI should modify its otherwise commendable Threat Review and Prioritization (TRP) process to make it more adaptable to emerging threats. It should incorporate judgments from long-term USIC forecasts and, to the extent that disagreement with these forecasts exists, this should be transparent in the TRP.

(U) Information Sharing

(U) Finding 5: Overall, the Review Commission found information sharing between the FBI and its federal, state, and local partners to be a "good news story." The situation today reflects the Bureau's strong commitment in recent years to improve collaboration with its key partners as well as their comparable response in the post-9/11 environment. But there is still room for improvement in the Bureau's sharing practices, especially with local law enforcement and the private sector. The case studies expose lapses in communication, coordination, and collaboration among Joint Terrorism Task Forces (JTTFs) in FBI field offices; between FBI Headquarters and the field; and between the Bureau and its federal, state, and local partners in law enforcement and intelligence.

(U) Recommendation 5: The Review Commission recommends that the FBI continue to reinforce and strengthen its communication, collaboration, and information-sharing practices with its federal, state, and local partners—including through the JTTFs—as a top priority in pursuit of its mission as the hub of US domestic intelligence. FBI progress on this issue and more detailed recommendations appear in Chapter IV. Specifically, the Review Commission recommends that the FBI:

- (U) The FBI should address the lingering perceptions among state and local law enforcement and other partners that it views relationships as transactional and tactical and is not interested in building lasting partnerships that advance common goals and missions; the Bureau should develop a strategy to address such perceptions head on.

- (U) Resolve the issues that prevent Task Force Officers (TFOs) from having full access to Guardian, Sentinel, and other sources so they can function as equal members of the Task Force; solutions should include mechanisms to alert TFOs and their FBI supervisors if anything has changed, that affects data base access.

- (U) Provide policy guidelines and a general framework to SACs that will assist them in decisions regarding real-time sharing of information with key local partners under defined circumstances. The implementation of this guidance should be included in field exercises that include FBI and local law enforcement.

- (U) In view of the above, the Review Commission recommends that the FBI continue to exploit advanced technology to ensure that state and local law enforcement get timely and useful feedback.

- (U) Establish a full-time position, filled by a qualified agent, to coordinate with the private sector or combine several part-time agents at each field office toward this end.

(U) Countering Violent Extremism (CVE)

(U) **Finding 6:** The Countering Violent Extremism Office's (CVEO's) current limited budget and fundamental law enforcement and intelligence responsibilities do not make it an appropriate vehicle for the social and prevention role in the CVE mission. Such initiatives are best undertaken by other government agencies.

(U) **Recommendation 6**: The Review Commission recommends that the primary social and prevention responsibilities for the CVE mission should be transferred from the FBI to the Department of Homeland Security (DHS) or distributed among other agencies more directly involved with community interaction.

(U) Legal Attachés (LEGAT) Program

(U) **Finding 7:** The challenges to the Bureau's core missions—criminal investigation, intelligence, and technology—are already and will be increasingly global. The Bureau's LEGAT program is growing—today's 64 LEGAT offices represent a three-fold increase since the early 1990s—and will need to continue to grow over the next decade.

- (U) They are a value proposition and wise investment for both criminal investigation and intelligence collection. But the various LEGAT offices exhibit marked differences in local missions, access, and capabilities.

- (U) The Bureau needs clearer goals for designating priority countries to assign LEGATs, for candidate selection, for enhanced training and education, for standardization of business processes, and especially for expanding analytic capability, including analysts embedded in the LEGAT offices.

- (U) The recently announced reorganization, developed by the International Operations Division (IOD), which includes such enhanced analytic capability, is encouraging as long as it receives commensurate resources.

(U) Recommendation 7: The Review Commission recommends that the Bureau match the growing mission of the LEGAT program with the level of resources needed to meet it, including commensurate funding to improve the analytic capability within IOD. The LEGAT program should be viewed as an integral part of field operations when allocating resources as opposed to its current role as an adjunct, support program.

- (U) To meet this enhanced role, IOD should standardize policies across the LEGAT offices. It should develop a strategic process to identify those countries most suitable for placement of LEGATs.

- (U) Candidate selection processes should be upgraded to ensure that positions are filled by the best qualified leaders to meet the particular mission needs. Each LEGAT's job in the field will vary but all will be involved in collaborative networks in which their grade, experience, and particular leadership skills will be key determinants of success.

- (U) Training and education programs should be enhanced to prepare LEGATs for their assignments. Rewarding career opportunities should be available for LEGAT personnel returning from successful overseas tours.

- (U) Intelligence support should be increased to the LEGATs. While the Review Commission does not recommend that every LEGAT automatically have an intelligence analyst overseas, such an improved capability could be achieved through designated "touch points" or temporary assignments.

(U) Science and Technology (S&T)

(U) Finding 8: The Review Commission sees rapidly advancing technologies affecting basic analytic and special agent tradecraft, the growing capabilities of adversaries, and new missions— including cyber and big data issues—for decades to come. The Bureau has substantially increased its investment in its S&T programs over the past decade, and has made strides in improving its S&T capabilities. It has committed to the DNI's goal to integrate intelligence community information technology (IT) architecture in a common platform Intelligence

Community Information Technology Enterprise (IC-ITE) for sharing information and technology.

- (U) The Review Commission heard informative briefings from the Bureau's Science and Technology Branch (Operational Technology Division, Laboratory Division, and Criminal Justice Information Services Division) on its bold efforts to keep apace of rapid advances in information technology, biometrics, DNA applications, forensics, and other sciences that relate to both the agent's investigative tradecraft and the adversary's capabilities.

(U) Recommendation 8: The FBI's S&T status quo, while commendable, is challenged to keep pace with a global technological revolution of unprecedented scale and scope. In its strategic planning, the FBI should regard S&T applications as a core competency for investment—including in selective research and development.

- (U) The Bureau should sustain its commitment to the DNI's program for IT integration, should develop closer relationships with USIC S&T centers, and should interact more with the National Academy of Sciences (NAS) —which can provide direct access for the FBI to scientists in any discipline. S&T managers should strongly encourage their scientists to participate in USIC and NAS meetings and projects.

- (U) The FBI's S&T Branch, while strengthening its outreach to the scientific community, also should increase its internal interaction or "touch points" within Headquarters, field offices, and LEGAT posts.

(U) Cyber Security

(U) Finding 9: The FBI Director has made cyber security a top national-security priority. He has stressed the growing threat to US interests from state and non-state actors who, working together or apart, are increasingly stealing US defense, intelligence, trade, and economic secrets, and who are maturing their capabilities to attack our critical infrastructure.

- (U) The Review Commission notes that the Bureau's Cyber Division is developing a comprehensive strategy to counter cyber-based attacks and to prevent and respond to high-technology crimes. There will be significant challenges for the FBI in implementing this strategy, especially in improving technology procurement practices, hiring expert personnel in a timely manner, and coordinating across government.

- (U) The National Cyber Investigative Joint Task Force (NCIJTF) and the 24/7 CyWatch are working toward better, real-time information sharing within the Bureau and with federal, state, and local partners. The FBI is getting high marks for its coordination and collaboration on cyber with other agencies, especially the National Security Agency (NSA).

114

- (U) The Bureau is challenged, however, by the continued lack of clarity regarding the respective roles and responsibilities of the various government actors. In particular, the FBI is challenged to rebuild constructive partnerships with the private sector and in the general public in the wake of the Snowden revelations and the decision of major telecommunications companies to opt for unbreakable encryption.

(U) Recommendations 9: The Review Commission commends the FBI on the cyber initiatives it has taken to date, but is concerned that its internal progress needs to be accelerated to meet a growing and potentially catastrophic threat. FBI leadership must quickly execute and accomplish technology, procurement, and personnel goals. The Bureau cannot succeed by itself. It requires Executive Branch leadership and must work with other agencies and the US Congress in what needs to be a government-wide collaborative effort.

- (U) The FBI Director should work with other agency heads and with the Congress on legislative initiatives to incentivize stronger partnerships with the private sector that enables private companies to communicate and work with the US government in countering cyber threats.

- (U) The FBI's Cyber Division should strengthen its internal coordination with other divisions, field offices and the LEGATs.

    - (U) The Cyber Division should closely coordinate and align priorities with the Human Resource Division to more effectively recruit the advanced technical skills it needs.

    - (U) The Cyber Division must efficiently collaborate with the S&T Branch to identify and effectively procure state-of-the art technologies required for its mission.

    - (U) The Cyber Division should accelerate its productive outreach to other agencies with important cyber security responsibilities.

(U) Legal Authorities and Civil Liberties

(U) Finding 10: The Review Commission's study of five recent, high-profile counterterrorism cases highlights the importance of the FBI's legal authorities to counter rapidly evolving national security threats.

- (U) The Electronic Communications Privacy Act (ECPA), Communications Assistance for Law Enforcement Act (CALEA), the Foreign Intelligence Surveillance Act (FISA), and the USA PATRIOT Act were all essential to the investigations in each case and are critical to the FBI's ability to counter the terrorist threat generally.

- (U) As the terrorism threat continues to evolve in the years ahead, Congress may need to expand and refine these authorities. At the same time, the Review Commission

115

recognizes that any expansion in the government's law enforcement and intelligence powers will raise civil liberties concerns in the Congress, among the American people, and within the FBI itself. These concerns will need to be addressed.

(U) Recommendation 10: The Review Commission recommends that Congress continue to provide the FBI with the authorities and state-of-the art tools it needs both to counter growing threats to US national security and to protect the freedoms of American citizens.

- (U) In this complex and dynamic environment, the Review Commission recommends that the FBI correspondingly continue to review, strengthen, and refine its internal safeguards for the protection of civil liberties. To this end, the FBI Director should establish an independent advisory group reporting directly to him to include several outside experts—technical, legal, and civic— to provide regular review of the effectiveness of existing safeguards and of the Bureau's compliance with them.

- (U) The goal should be to make the Director aware of potential problems in time to fix them, before they become real problems that he learns of from the Department of Justice (DOJ) Inspector General, a whistleblower, or the media.

(U) Strategic Plan

(U) Finding 11: The effort to develop a long-term comprehensive strategic vision and plan to integrate the national and international responsibilities of a global intelligence-driven investigative service is complicated by some problems that the Bureau can fix on its own, but others will require the involvement of DOJ, DNI, and Congress.

- (U) Strategic planning is hindered by the Bureau's one-year budget cycle, which contrasts with the five-year cycle of most USIC members who are funded by the defense budget. The bifurcated budget process runs through the contrasting evaluations of DOJ and FBI's Office of the Director of National Intelligence budget offices and eventually on to the Congressional committees of jurisdiction, which are similarly divided between intelligence and law enforcement interests.

(U) Recommendation 11: The Review Commission recommends that the FBI develop a comprehensive strategic vision—and a five-year, implementable, metric-based strategic plan— that would integrate its expanding national and global missions, as well as its intelligence and law enforcement mandates.

- (U) The FBI's strategic planning must be top-down, comprehensive, long term, and done in close coordination with the DNI, the Attorney General, the Office of Management and Budget, and Congressional committees of jurisdiction. All these stakeholders must be more aligned in their commitment to the Bureau's critical mission to integrate intelligence and law enforcement.

- (U) The strategic plan under the Director's leadership should integrate division-level strategic plans, drive allocation of resources, direct support functions, and track with a dynamic, multi-year threat assessment.

- (U) The plan must enable the professionalization of FBI analysis, improvement in the HUMINT program, long-term strengthening of the LEGAT program, and the acceleration of S&T initiatives.

- (U) The Director's plan should aim to upgrade over time the Bureau's key business processes—including information technology, human resources, security, contracting, and procurement.

(U) Continued Investigation of 9/11 Attack

(U) Finding 12: The FBI has continued to investigate the 9/11 attacks to determine whether any additional individuals should be held responsible for the attacks. Although the additional evidence uncovered since the 9/11 Commission report strengthens the cases against already identified co-conspirators, the Review Commission finds there is no new evidence to date that would change the 9/11 Commission's findings regarding responsibility for the 9/11 attacks. Contrary to media reports, the FBI did not have a source in the 1990's with direct access to UBL nor was there credible evidence linking the Sarasota, Florida, family to the 9/11 hijackers.

(U) Recommendation 12: The 9/11 Review Commission recommends the FBI continue its thorough investigation into the 9/11 attacks and, after the trials of the conspirators conclude, capture the lessons learned through the investigation, and provide detailed briefings to Director Comey and the relevant congressional oversight committees.

(U) CONCLUSION

(U) In conclusion, the FBI has made strides in the past decade but needs to accelerate its implementation of reforms to complete its transformation into a threat-based, intelligence-driven organization. The increasingly complex and dangerous threat environment it faces will require no less. The Review Commission believes that the FBI's vision of the future should be one in which criminal investigation, counterintelligence, intelligence collection and analysis, and S&T applications are seen as complementary core competencies of a global intelligence and investigative agency.

- (U) The Bureau must work toward a culture that integrates its best efforts into both criminal and national security missions; where its highly skilled people intersect synergistically in mission support; but where its core competencies still are nurtured by distinct professional disciplines requiring their own investment strategies, specialized training, and discipline-managed career services.

- (U) The FBI will fulfill its domestic intelligence role when its analysts and collectors, like its special agents, are grounded in criminal investigation; have ready access to state-of-the-art technology; continuously exploit the systems, tools, and relationships of the national intelligence agencies; and both cultivate and benefit from robust CONUS and OCONUS collaborative relationships that widen the Bureau's access to investigative leads and reportable intelligence.

- (U) Achieving these ambitious goals should not be a zero-sum game between intelligence and law enforcement. It should mean a continued FBI commitment to a growing criminal investigation mission, to a tighter and smoother integration of intelligence analysts and collectors into the USIC, to a more strategic approach to its growing international footprint, and to greater investment in closer collaborative relationships with US and foreign partners. Accomplishing all this will be hard in any case, but impossible without a firm commitment from FBI leadership and support from the DNI and Congress to accelerate reform.

(U) APPENDIX

(U) Appendix A: Briefs Provided by FBI Headquarters' Divisions

(U) Briefing Title

9/11 Additional Evidence
9/11 Background brief
9/11 Investigation Overview
Sarasota Family
Anwar Al-Aulaqi Part I
Anwar al-Aulaqi Part II
Countering Violent Extremism
Cyber Dark Turist and Inspired Calm Brief
Cyber Strategic Plan
Cyber Texas Model Demonstration
David Headley
DI Employee Development brief
DI Inspection Report
DI Strategic Plan
Disruptions of Attempted Terrorist Attacks
EAD-1 Update
Evolution of the National Security Branch
Faisal Shahzad
FBI Leadership Briefing
Foreign Language Program
Fort Hood/Nidal Hassan
Going Dark Brief
Guardian/eGuardian Briefing
Homegrown Violent Extremists Survey
Integrated Training for Agents & Analysts – Integrated Curriculum Initiative
Intel Products/Dissemination
IOD Americas Unit Brief
IOD Briefings on Asia Legats
IOD Europe Unit Brief
JTTFs
Language Services
Legat Ankara
LEGAT Meeting - Abu Dhabi
LEGAT Meeting - Tel Aviv
Meeting with Mike Steinbach
Moner Abusalha Brief
Moner Abusalha Brief - Part II
Najibullah Zazi

(U) Appendix B: Interviews Conducted by the 9/11 Review Commission

(U) Name	(U) Title/Position
John MacGaffin	Former CIA Deputy NCS (DO), FBI rotation
Maureen Baginski	Former FBI EAD, NSA Senior
Seamus Hughes	NCTC, former Senate HSGA committee
Philip Mudd	Former FBI Deputy NSB, CIS Senior
George Salameh	NSS Staff CVE
Charles Allen	Former DHS Undersecretary, CIA Senior
Gabriel Weimann	Professor of Communication at the Department of Communication at Haifa University, Israel
Jerome P. Bjelopera	Congressional Research Staffer
Harvey Rishikof	Chair of the Advisory Committee for the American Bar Association Standing Committee on Law and National Security
Michael Leiter	Former Director of the National Counterterrorism Center (NCTC)
Christopher Kojm	Chairman of the National Intelligence Council
Michael German	Brennan Center for Justice
Kenneth Wainstein	Former General Counsel and Chief of Staff to the FBI Director
David Pekoske & Kathleen Kiernan	InfraGard Chairmen
John Pistole	Administrator of the United States Transportation Security Administration
Henry Hollatz	Director of NCTC/Directorate of Intelligence
Robert Newton	Deputy of NCTC/Directorate for Strategic Operational Planning (DSOP)
Glen Fine	Former Inspector General, Department of Justice
Kshemendra Paul	Program Manager for Information Sharing Environment (PM-ISE)
James Dinkins	Former Executive Associate Director of Homeland Security Investigations (HIS) for Immigration and Customs Enforcement (ICE)
Dawn Scalici and James Blasingame	National Intelligence Manager for Western Hemisphere and Homeland and her Deputy, James Blasingame
Bassem Youseff	Former FBI Special Agent
Christopher Inglis	Former Deputy Director of National Security Agency (NSA)
Robert Mueller	Former FBI Director
James Clapper	Director of National Intelligence
Francis Taylor	Undersecretary for Intelligence and Analysis (I&A), Department of Homeland Security (DHS)
Gil Kerlikowski	Commissioner for Customs & Border Protection (CBP)
David Shedd	Acting Director of the Defense Intelligence Agency (DIA)
Theodore Nicholas	Assistant Director of the National Intelligence for Partner Engagement at the Office of the Director of National Intelligence
Patrick Reynolds	NSA NCR Representative
Michael Flynn	Former Director of the Defense Intelligence Agency (DIA)
John Brennan	Director of the Central Intelligence Agency (CIA)

(U) Appendix C: Select FBI Intelligence Program Developments Since 2005[361]

(U) Initiative	(U) Year
Established Intelligence Sections at FBI HQ	2002-2009
Created the National Security Branch	2005
Established the Directorate of Intelligence (DI)	2005
Established the Intelligence Analyst Advisory Board	2005
Deployed Permanent Intelligence Analysts overseas at LEGATS	2006
Created the FBI Director's Daily Brief briefer position	2006
Piloted the Domain Management Initiative	2006
Created the DI Desk Officer Program	2007
Established the Strategic Execution Team (SET)	2007
Began appointing Senior Intelligence Officers	2007
Established the DI HUMINT Operations Section	2007
Created the Chief Information Sharing Officer position	2008
Began an FBI Open Source program	2008
Created Senior Supervisory Intelligence Analyst positions	2009
Launched the Language Services Management System	2009
Created the Senior Intelligence Officer Council	2009
Developed Threat Mitigation Teams	2009
Established a Collection Management Program	2009
Developed first National Threat Priorities list	2009
Established Counterterrorism Fusion Cells	2010
Developed the Fusion Center Engagement Strategy	2010
Created the DI Executive Intelligence Section	2010
Initiated direct dissemination of raw intelligence	2010
Created an intelligence analyst career path model	2010
Established the HUMINT Advisory Council	2011
Developed the Intelligence Workforce Strategy	2011
Created Intelligence Program Manager positions	2012
Established Fusion Cells in the operations divisions	2012
Instituted the Domestic DNI Representative program	2012
Built the Intelligence Analyst Training Center at Quantico	2012
Created Deputy Assistant Directors for Intelligence	2012
Launched the Intelligence Portal	2012
Established the Threat Review and Prioritization Process	2013
Developed the Integrated Curriculum Initiative	2014

---

[361] This list is a representative sample of FBI developments regarding its intelligence program since 2005 and does not encompass all intelligence initiatives.

Established the Intelligence Branch	2014
Created the DI Intelligence Workforce Development Section	2014

(U) Appendix D: Acronyms Found in This Report

Al-Nusra	Jabhat al-Nusra in Syria
ALAT	Assistant Legal Attaches
AQI	Al Qa'ida in Iraq
AODP	Agent Operational Designation Program
AOR	Area of Responsibility
AQAP	al-Qa'ida in the Arabian Peninsula
AQIM	al-Qa'ida in the Islamic Maghreb
AS	al-Shabaab in Somalia
ASAC	Assistant Special Agent in Charge
BFTC	Basic Field Training Course
BSS	British Security Service
CALEA	Communications Assistance for Law Enforcement Act
CBP	Customs and Border Protection
CBR	Chemical, Biological, and Radiological
CBRN	Chemical, Biological, Radiological, and Nuclear
CCTF	Common Cyber Threat Framework
CD	Counterintelligence Division
CDC	Cleared Defense Contractors
CEPDU	Continuing Education and Professional Development Unit
CHOU	Counterterrorism HUMINT Operations Unit
CHS	Confidential Human Source
CIA	Central Intelligence Agency
CID	Criminal Investigative Division
CJSR	Commerce, Justice, Science and Related Agencies Subcommittee
CONUS	Continental United States
COS	Chief of Station
CPI	Crime Problem Indicator
CSCC	Central Strategic Coordinating Component
CSG	Consolidated Strategy Guide
CTC	Counterterrorism Center
CTD	Counterterrorism Division
CTT	Cyber Threat Team
CVE	Countering Violent Extremism
CVEO	Countering Violent Extremism Office
CYD	Cyber Division
DCI	Director of Central Intelligence
DCIS	Defense Criminal Investigative Service
DEA	Drug Enforcement Administration
DHS	Department of Homeland Security
DI	Directorate of Intelligence
DIA	Defense Intelligence Agency
DINs	Domain Intelligence Notes
DIOG	Domestic Operations Investigative Guide

DNI	Directorate of National Intelligence
DOD	Department of Defense
DOJ	Department of Justice
DSAC	Domestic Security Alliance Council
DSOP	Directorate of Strategic Operational Planning
EAD	Executive Assistant Director
EC	Electronic Communication
ECPA	Electronic Communications Privacy Act
FBI	Federal Bureau of Investigation
FBIHQ	FBI Headquarters
FIG	Field Intelligence Group
FIOC	FBI Intelligence Officer Certification
FISA	Foreign Intelligence Surveillance Act
FISC	Foreign Intelligence Surveillance Court
FOSP	Field Office Strategic Plan
FSB	Federal Security Service
FTTTF	Foreign Terrorist Tracking Task Force
FY	Fiscal Year
GAO	Government Accountability Office
HIG	High-Value Detainee Interrogation Group
HRD	Human Resources Division
HSI	Homeland Security Investigation
HUMINT	Human Intelligence
HVE	Homegrown Violent Extremist
I&A	Intelligence and Analysis
IA	Intelligence Analyst
IAWS	Intelligence Analyst Workforce Study
IB	Intelligence Branch
IC-ITE	Intelligence Community Information Technology Enterprise
ICATEC	Intelligence Community Analysis Traning and Education Council
ICE	Immigration and Customs Enforcement
ICI	Integrated Curriculum Initiative
IED	Improvised Explosive Device
IIR	Intelligence Information Report
IOD	International Operations Division
IPM	Integrated Program Management
IPMT	Integrated Program Management Tool
IRTPA	Intelligence Reform and Terrorism Prevention Act
ISI	Inter-Services Intelligence
ISIL	Islamic State of Iraq and the Levant
IT	Information Technology
ITN	Identification, Tasking, and Networking
ITOS I	International Terrorist Organizations Section I
ITOS II	International Terrorist Organizations Section II
ITOS	International Terrorism Operations Section

JRIG	Joint Regional Intelligence Group
JTTF	Joint Terrorism Task Force
KCIC	Kurdish Community Islamic Center
KSM	Khalid Shaykh Muhammad
LEGAT	Legal Attachés
LEICLO	Law Enforcement and Intelligence Liaison Office
LET	Lashkar-e-Tayyiba
MCCA	Major Cities Chiefs Association
MOU	Memorandum of Understanding
NADP	New Agent Development Program
NAPA	National Academy of Public Administration
NCIS	Naval Criminal Investigative Service
NCTC	National Counterterrorism Center
NGA	National Geospatial-Intelligence Agency
NIC	National Intelligence Council
NIE	National Intelligence Estimate
NIMA	National Imagery and Mapping Agency
NIP	National Intelligence Program
NIPB	National Intelligence Producers Board
NIPF	National Intelligence Priorities Framework
NIU	National Intelligence University
NJTTF	National Joint Terrorism Task Force
NR	National Resources
NRO	National Reconnaissance Office
NSA	National Security Agency
NSB	National Security Branch
NSL	National Security Letter
NSD	National Security Division
NSLB	National Security Law Branch
NYO	New York Office
NYPD	New York Police Department
OCONUS	Outside the Continental United States
ODNI	Office of the Director of National Intelligence
PDDNI	Principal Deputy Director of National Intelligence's
POA	Program of Analysis
R & D	Research and Development
RSO	Regional Security Officer
S & T	Science and Technology
SAC	Special Agent in Charge
SAR	Suspicious Activity Report
SCIF	Sensitive Compartmental Information Facilities
SET	Strategic Executive Team
SIGINT	Signals Intelligence
SNIO	Senior National Intelligence Officers
SOS	Staff Operations Specialist

SSA	Supervisory Special Agent
STAS	Special Technologies and Applications Section
SWE	Secure Work Environment
TAREX	Target Exploitation
TExAS Tool	Threat Examination and Scoping Tool
TFO	Task Force Officer
TMS	Threat Mitigation Strategy
TMTs	Threat Mitigation Teams
TRP	Threat Review and Prioritization
TSA	Transportation Security Administration
TSC	Terrorist Screening Center
TTIC	Terrorist Threat Integration Center
TTP	Tehrik-e Taliban Pakistan
TURK	Time Utilization and Recordkeeping
UBL	Usama bin Laden
US	United States
USG	United States Government
USIC/IC	United States Intelligence Community/ Intelligence Community
VCF	Virtual Case File
VEO	Violent Extremist Organizations
WAII	Warning and Anticipatory Intelligence Initiative
WMD	Weapons of Mass Destruction
WMDD	Weapons of Mass Destruction Directorate
WMDP	Weapons of Mass Destruction Program

www.ingramcontent.com/pod-product-compliance
Lightning Source LLC
Chambersburg PA
CBHW081837250726
48659CB00008B/2483